"You are the parent. If you can change and do what this wonderful book invites you to change and do, then you can give the most precious gift to your child—transforming your child's "problem" into a strength. Please accept the gift of this book—for your child's sake."

—*Alvin R. Mahrer, Ph.D., professor emeritus of psychology at the University of Ottawa, Canada, and author of* The Complete Guide to Experiential Psychotherapy

"Honos-Webb grabbed my scattered attention quickly and held it with this enlightening book, without resorting to drugs. I nervously jumped to sections such as 'The Medical Model of Disease' and 'Why Medications May Not Be the Answer' and found them balanced and enlightening. Then I calmed down, read the rest, and learned a lot. You will too . . . if you can pay attention."

—*Thomas Greening, professor of psychology at Saybrook Graduate School and editor of the* Journal of Humanistic Psychology

"Honos-Webb's book is a healing gift to children with ADHD and their parents, teachers, psychologists, and doctors. Taken to heart, her message could transform the lives of these children, their families, and even the educational system. *The Gift of ADHD* is a must-read for anyone whose life is touched by the unique children who are given this diagnosis. Even adults with this diagnosis should read this book to find a radically new way of understanding themselves and celebrating their own gifts."

—*Lane Arye, Ph.D., author of* Unintentional Music: Releasing Your Deepest Creativity *and internationally known process-oriented therapist and teacher*

the Gift of ADHD

SECOND EDITION

How to Transform Your Child's Problems into Strengths

LARA HONOS-WEBB, PH.D.

New Harbinger Publications, Inc.

Publisher's Note

Distributed in Canada by Raincoast Books

Copyright © 2010 by Lara Honos-Webb
New Harbinger Publications, Inc.
5674 Shattuck Avenue
Oakland, CA 94609
www.newharbinger.com

All Rights Reserved
Printed in the United States of America

Acquired by Tesilya Hanauer; Cover design by Amy Shoup;
Edited by Karen O'Donnell Stein; Text design by Tracy Marie Carlson

Library of Congress Cataloging-in-Publication Data

Honos-Webb, Lara.
  The gift of ADHD : how to transform your child's problems into strengths / Lara Honos-Webb ; foreword by Scott M. Shannon. -- 2nd ed.
    p. cm.
  Includes bibliographical references.
  ISBN 978-1-57224-850-2
  1. Attention-deficit hyperactivity disorder--Popular works. I. Title. II. Title: Gift of attention deficit hyperactivity disorder.
  RJ506.H9H66 2010
  618.92'8589--dc22

                              2010016100

16 15 14

10 9 8 7 6

Contents

Acknowledgments

I gratefully dedicate this book to Ken, Kenny, and Audrey Webb for giving me the gift of waking up happy every day.

I thank my brother, John Honos, and my mother, Karen Honos, for giving me a front-row seat, allowing me to understand ADHD as a gift. John's unique gifts and my mother's unique approach are the inspiration for this book. Thanks also to Edward, Chrissty, Grace, Cate, and Luke Honos for being my cheerleaders along the way. I also appreciate the support from and interesting conversations with Carole and Bill Webb and Anna and Rosie Chalfant.

This book owes much to the scholarly work of Larry Leitner, whose pioneering work on humanistic assessment is the primary scholarly inspiration for the approach taken herein.

I also want to thank my acquisitions editor, Tesilya Hanauer, for her incredible support throughout the process and for her initial interest in my work. Thank you for seeing so much potential in my views on ADHD and in my work. I am also grateful for the thorough editorial assistance of Heather Mitchener, Carole Honeychurch, and Karen Stein.

So much of this book was shaped by stimulating conversations with friends and colleagues Marc Celentana, Cy Estonactac, Jenny Yeaggy, Rose Pacini, and Jeannie Lopez. Thanks to Kimberly McCoy for her special insights and sharing of personal experiences. I am grateful for the encouragement and support from Dr. Robin Goldstein and Annemarie Roeper. I appreciate like-minded colleagues including Dr. Scott Shannon, Barbara Probst, and Daniel Pink. I want to thank Lema Almaddine for her research assistance. I'm grateful to Hagen Panton for his helpful conversations and idea to create a "When the Teacher Calls" list for parents.

Many thanks are due to Dick and Alison Jones and their family for their remarkable generosity of spirit, and I thank John Thomas for his lifelong support and encouragement.

Finally, I am grateful to William Cangemi and Elizabeth Harrick for their original interest in the research project that led to this book.

Foreword

Attention Deficit Hyperactivity Disorder (ADHD) is a common and difficult challenge for children and young adults. This disorder affects boys much more often than girls and has continued to increase in rates over the last three decades. In the 1970's there were about 250,000 children identified with this problem. Today, we have almost four million youth labeled with this diagnosis and over two million treated with stimulant medications. The United States uses about 80% of the world's stimulant medications. Rates of diagnosis in other countries are a small fraction of what we diagnose here in America. What is going on here?

In 2007 Phillip Shaw, MD and his colleagues at National Institute of Mental Health published a groundbreaking study of ADHD. They took brain scans of 446 kids (with and without ADHD) over many years and monitored brain development. This is the by far the largest study of pediatric brain development in ADHD. What they found was remarkable: there was NO evidence of brain abnormality in the children with ADHD, only developmental delay. This echoes an earlier panel selected to explore this topic a few years previously. National Institute of Health convened a panel of the country's experts in a variety of related fields to discuss whether ADHD was a biological illness or not. After exploring all of the research on this topic this panel decided that they could not determine if ADHD was an illness or merely at the far end of normal development. They also expressed concern that we have no clear ideas about the cause or prevention of ADHD.

For many years I have been trying to educate the public and members of my own profession about these issues. ADHD represents a common collection of symptoms that can be triggered by a variety of factors: iron deficiency, thyroid problems, poor diet, inadequate sleep, head injury, allergies, excessive early television, environmental toxins and any more controllable or treatable concerns.

If we accept the scientifically based perspective that ADHD is a symptom rather than an illness we are then empowered to take charge of this situation. We can alter the problems in the child's life and improve their focus, attention and capacity to learn. Otherwise we hold a view that the child has brain damage via faulty genetics and imbalanced neurochemistry. There is little else parents can do if they embrace this perspective other than medicate their child indefinitely.

I reject that view and I encourage you to as well. I would embrace the view that your child has strengths and challenges in their make up. We all must hold the ecologically sound viewpoint that all things are interconnected and interdependent. As part of the ecological or holistic perspective many different facets of the child's life can affect their mental and physical well being. As a parent and a culture we must acknowledge that many aspects of our lives can support or deteriorate a child's abilities and health. Once we do that we can begin to see how we can help or harm our child by the choices that we make each and every day.

Each young person must be seen as a vibrant and adaptable being capable of wondrous change and growth. One of the most defining characteristics of childhood is the neuro-plasticity found within their central nervous system. This means that the young brain can change, adapt and grow in response to their environment. This includes their home life, emotional support, intellectual stimulation, proper nutrition, viewed media, social supports, spiritual path and academic fit among others.

Fifty years from now people will laugh at the diagnosis of ADHD and shudder at the liberal use of stimulant medication in young children. Instead we need to move towards a strength-based approach that builds on the gifts and talents of each child. We must support the child as needed but fully embrace their ability to grow and change in a positive manner.

I am honored to write this forward for Lara Honos-Webb as I think she has embodied this message in her work. This book is filled with hope and promise for everyone concerned with the diagnosis of ADHD. Rather than view ADHD as a negative psychiatric illness, she has chosen to see that this concern comes with many strengths and possibilities. See this book as a blessing that will help you as you move through life. Thank you Lara for your message of hope.

—Scott Shannon, MD
   Assistant Clinical Professor of Child Psychiatry
   University of Colorado
   Children's Hospital
   Denver, Colorado

Preface to the Second Edition

What if you defined yourself by what you are good at rather than by what you are not good at? What if you asked, "What went right?" instead of "What went wrong?" What if you believed that those talents that come easily to you were your greatest gifts? Now ask yourself those same questions about your child. Can you imagine the momentum you would generate if you called your child "an innovative problem solver" rather than "someone who stinks at math"? It may seem difficult to believe, but the motivation and confidence you gain through defining your child by his or her gifts can make it easier for your child to plow through weaknesses—lack of focus, difficulty paying attention to details, impulsiveness, or lack of stick-to-it-iveness.

I've always been amazed that, though the terms "ADD" and "ADHD" are bandied about like the latest fad in some circles (and are like a life sentence in other circles), only a few people ask a very important question, which is fundamental to a disorder defined by an attention deficit.

That question is "What is attention?" If you are awake you are paying attention to lots of things, all the time. So how can someone have a deficit of attention? Upon further examination, we may realize that an attention deficit is really a case of not paying attention to what you are *supposed to* be paying attention to. Many diagnoses of children with attention-deficit/hyperactivity disorder (ADHD) result from a child not paying attention in school or to their parents.

Imagine a child who does not play basketball very well. We notice this child's difficulty with the game, and we give him the label "basketball deficit disorder." But what if we asked ourselves, "How can I increase his skill in playing basketball?" We know that the answer lies in increasing his skills through coaching and practice. Now consider the child who has difficulty paying attention. I wonder how different things would be if, when we first noticed a child not paying attention to an assigned task, we paused before issuing the ADHD label. And what if, in that pause, we asked ourselves, "How do we increase this child's attention?"

Just as we can increase basketball skills through coaching and practice, we can increase attention through coaching and practice. In this second edition of *The Gift of ADHD*, you will find many methods of increasing attention that did not appear in the first edition. These techniques include various forms of meditation and one of the newest rages in the field of psychology, "brain fitness training," originally developed for the treatment of aging in the brain. This technique's potential for application with ADHD is obvious and ripe for exploration.

Besides skills, there is another facet of attention, which we all know from personal experience: interest. We pay attention to what we are interested in.

If you want to increase a child's attention, find out what he is interested in and use that as rocket fuel to propel an increase in attention. It's a simple formula that gives a child a chance at something other than a label that stings.

Too many times, my desk is stacked with psychiatric evaluations that can be summarized like this: "Age ten, diagnosis ADHD. Age twelve, diagnosis ADHD and major depression. Age fourteen, ADHD and cannabis dependence." We can't deny that giving a child a deficit-disorder label can impair confidence and motivation. But there is another way.

Once, when I was a guest on a radio show, the host said about my book, *The Gift of ADHD*, "So what's the big deal? We all know that if we go to work and our boss tells us we are doing a good job we will feel good about ourselves and try harder." Although this might seem like he was trivializing my book, I had never heard sweeter words. He was absolutely right—it *is* obvious.

I don't mean that it's easy, however. I've gotten e-mails from parents telling me, "If you knew my kids you wouldn't call it a gift." If you cannot look at it as a gift, then perhaps you can see it as an opportunity for intervention. Consider that you are likely to get more of what you focus on. If you focus on the deficit disorder, you are likely to get more deficit. If you focus on gifts, you're likely to get more positive results. It doesn't work as quickly as medication, but it could change a person's life, and it would certainly have the positive side effects of increasing confidence and motivation.

In the five years since the first edition of *The Gift of ADHD* was released, much of what was in the book has gone mainstream. Research has emerged that supports the idea of spaciness being a gift related to both creativity and interpersonal skill. Ecological consciousness, the most marginalized of all the ideas in the first edition, has been listed by *Time* magazine as one of "ten ideas changing the world right now" (Walsh 2009). *Last Child in the Woods: Saving Our Children from Nature-Deficit Disorder*, by Richard Louv (2005), a book released at about the same time as *The Gift of ADHD*, spurred national movements including one named "No Child Left Inside."

The research on the attention-boosting benefits of spending time in nature has shown that nature is medicine.

The largest nationally funded study (MTA Study Group 2009) on the effects of medication to treat ADHD reached the conclusion that, though medication works quickly and in the short term, after eight years the benefits for those who initially received medication are not different from the benefits of treatment without medication. Even years ago, any neuropsychologist would probably have told you that the brain will habituate to medication treatment, and now the state-of-the-art, nationally funded research tells us the same. The conclusion of the biggest study with the longest follow-up and leading experts is that we need to develop new and additional treatments for ADHD.

This book does offer a new treatment approach. It's an approach that builds on the very latest developments in neuropsychology, positive psychology, personality psychology, developmental psychology, and my own field, clinical psychology. The most exciting development in our understanding of the brain is in the area of *neuroplasticity*, which simply means that we can change our brains. So, before we label our children, why don't we start by encouraging them to take advantage of the newly discovered fact that the harder they try, the more they can change their brain.

Preface to the
First Edition

If each historical period comes with its own popular diagnoses, then ADHD would be a likely candidate for a diagnosis that characterizes our society at this point in history. One can hardly watch a television show or read a popular magazine without seeing an advertisement for a new or improved medication for treating children diagnosed with this disorder.

With all the attention this disorder has received in the popular press recently, the label of ADHD has taken on a power of its own. Media outlets would have us believe that ADHD has grown to epidemic proportions. Researchers estimate that 3 to 7 percent of all school-aged children have been given the diagnosis of ADHD (American Psychiatric Association 2000). ADHD is three times more likely to be diagnosed in boys than in girls (Barkley 2000). Estimates indicate that the rates of diagnosis of ADHD have increased 400 percent since 1988 (Stein 1999), although the explosion of this disorder seems confined to the United States. Some experts suggest that the increase indicates increasing misdiagnosis. As developmental specialist Robin Goldstein writes, "Parents and teachers worried by the increase in ADD need to know that there are a variety of other, more common reasons why a young child would have trouble listening to adults or paying attention to his responsibilities" (Goldstein 2002, 163). Dr. Goldstein points to some clear guidelines for addressing these reasons, including finding more flexible day-care arrangements, limiting TV, and making discipline a priority.

As a parent of a child with ADHD, you may find comfort that you are not alone in facing the recent explosion of information, services, and medications aimed at treating ADHD. You may also feel confused by so much information, much of it contradictory.

WHAT IS ADHD?

The term *ADHD* is often used in an offhand manner to describe children who seem to be out of control. However, it is actually a diagnosis that requires many specific criteria in order to be met. The two major dimensions of ADHD, according to the *Diagnostic and Statistical Manual of Mental Disorders* (American Psychiatric Association 2000), are inattention and hyperactivity/impulsivity.

The behavioral symptoms of inattention include making careless mistakes, being easily distracted, and having a difficult time completing projects. Other behavioral manifestations of inattention include difficulty listening, difficulty following directions, and difficulty with organization; a person may often lose homework and other things, run late, or forget appointments.

The symptoms of hyperactivity include fidgeting, difficulty sitting still, excessive talking, and difficulty doing quiet activities. Children with hyperactivity often feel as if they are being driven by a motor. Symptoms of impulsivity include blurting out inappropriate comments, being unable to wait for one's turn, and acting without thinking.

Although many children display some of these symptoms some of the time, a diagnosis of ADHD requires that there be evidence that these symptoms are severe enough to impair functioning in more than one setting. Usually this means that the child is disruptive both in a school setting and at home. Furthermore, a diagnosis of ADHD requires that other possible disorders be ruled out. For example, a child who is anxious, depressed, or oppositional may have many symptoms that look like ADHD. However, if the symptoms are better explained by another diagnosis, ADHD will not be given as a diagnosis.

A diagnosis of ADHD requires a thorough assessment and usually entails testing and collecting information from children, parents, and teachers. Because the diagnosis requires evidence that the behavioral disruptions occur in more than one setting, teachers and parents play an important role in a formal assessment process.

If your child has been given a diagnosis of ADHD without a very thorough assessment involving parents and teachers, you may want to consider getting a second opinion. Because the diagnosis may have an impact on your child's expectations and feelings of self-worth, you want to be sure that a thorough evaluation has been conducted by a trained professional.

WHOM THIS BOOK IS FOR, AND HOW IT'S DIFFERENT

This book is intended for parents of children who are six to twelve years old and have been diagnosed with ADHD by a trained professional. It is written for parents who are interested in transforming not only their child's symptoms but also their own vision of what ADHD means. Even if your child's ADHD diagnosis came as a relief, because it seemed to answer many of your questions about your child's behavior, this book will be helpful to you. A child with

ADHD is different from other children in predictable ways, and this book will help you to see that though your child's differences pose many challenges they also offer many gifts. So whether you were happy, relieved, distressed, or distraught when your child was diagnosed with ADHD, this book will guide you toward transforming your vision of your child—as well as your relationship with your child and his symptoms.

Many books for helping children and parents with ADHD offer very complicated, labor-intensive exercises for parents and children to do. These are not so helpful because children, and sometimes parents, have difficulty completing and following through with complex plans and long, drawn-out exercises. This book is different because it recognizes that an effective treatment plan has to match the difference that your child exhibits. In fact, the techniques in the book are designed to cater to your child's differences. They will use his need for concrete sensory engagement rather than abstract theorizing as a strategy for learning new information. Also, many of the exercises ask you to build on your child's areas of specialized interest and enthusiasm, whether it's Harry Potter or *American Idol*. You will help your child channel his existing energy for special interests into pretend games that transform his symptoms.

As you go through the book, keep in mind that there are more than enough exercises throughout to help transform your child's problems into strengths. If you or your child doesn't like some of the exercises, don't push it. Just move on to another exercise. The best strategy will be to find a handful of exercises that your child enjoys—the ones that are so much fun that they seem like playing— and to use those exercises over time. You can think of this approach as similar to going to the gym to build muscles. The more your child learns how to manage his thoughts, behaviors, and sense of self-worth, the more powerful his transformation will be. These exercises are not just one more thing that pits you and your child against each other. Rather, they will be fun activities for you and your child to share, and they will help you build your relationship and closeness with each other.

ADHD AS A GIFT: A PARADIGM SHIFT

This book will offer you not just information but rather a radical new way of looking at your child's diagnosis: although your child is different, the constellation of traits labeled as ADHD is in fact a gift. To go from seeing your child as having a deficit disorder to seeing your child as having a unique gift would be a major shift that would help both you and your child.

This radical way of looking at your child and his differences will be the starting point for a program of change that will help you shift from being your child's apologist to being your child's advocate. As an apologist for your child, you may have accepted the critical comments of his teachers and felt like you had to apologize for his behavior. As an advocate for your child, you will learn to gently challenge the teacher's criticism and reframe your child's behavior in a more positive light, providing the teacher with helpful suggestions for handling your child's differences.

At first you may greet this positive reframing of ADHD as welcome news, but you may also find it difficult to believe—because perhaps your child's teachers, pediatrician, and psychiatrist have all told you that your child has a serious problem. It can be very difficult to consider that all these experts might be wrong. You may have even found yourself frustrated with your child's behavior and lack of motivation and perhaps feeling relieved to know that there is a name for your child's problems.

The many educators and health professionals you have encountered are not necessarily wrong; your child is indeed different, just different in a way that our culture has not learned to fully appreciate. They are also correct in their observations that some problematic behaviors have emerged. Where they may not be entirely right is in their view of these differences—they may be seeing the differences as elements that define your child rather than as potential gifts and opportunities. And they may have failed to notice the ways in which the diagnosis of ADHD itself can cause problems in behavior, attention, and motivation. This book will help reveal how your child's differences have a lot to offer, both to him and to the world.

My first encounter with ADHD occurred when my own brother was diagnosed with it, long before it was a popular diagnosis or even a widely known condition. My mother never understood my brother's ADHD as a disorder. She regaled us with stories about how intuitive my brother was and how sensitive he was to people's emotions. We all noticed it. As a family, we saw that, although he often burst out with irreverent comments about the people we encountered, he was amazingly perceptive. When my mother reluctantly agreed to put him on medication, she viewed it as a concession to particular teachers who had complained about my brother in the classroom. She also found that whether he "needed" the medication or not depended on the teacher he had that year. Some years he would need the medication, but other years, he would do well and did not need medication at school. It was my mother's understanding that the medication was a means of appeasing others. For example, she would give my brother his medication when her own mother came to visit. My grandmother had a hard time tolerating my brother's rambunctious behavior; as a result, my mom would give the medication to my brother so my grandmother would not get so disturbed.

As a clinical psychologist I have spent years training to be sensitive to other people's emotions and to understand interpersonal interactions. Despite all my training, I have found that my brother's ability to capture the complexities of interpersonal interactions and other people's emotional states far surpasses my own—and the abilities of many of my well-trained colleagues. He possesses an interpersonal intuition that no amount of training could bestow.

It's true that children with ADHD have a keen ability to perceive insincerity and are not fooled by people's efforts to appear to be something they are not. Certainly, this represents a gift of interpersonal intuition, but you can see that, without some training in how to use this gift, it can create relationship problems for your ADHD child, who may be prone to making irreverent or inappropriate comments based on his perceptions.

The Frustration of Being Misunderstood

The following is a example of what typically happens to children with ADHD in treatment settings.

Jack was a seven-year-old patient in a child and adolescent psychiatric unit. One day, as he was sitting in a session of group therapy, Jack noticed that the nurse running the session seemed to have a permanently sour expression and was treating the young group members with disdain. She displayed little compassion for the struggles the patients were facing.

Jack, who had been given the diagnosis of ADHD, was making faces at her—in some way mirroring her sour expression but amplifying it. He was not deliberately trying to be disrespectful and perhaps wasn't even aware of the effect of his behavior—he was just naturally mirroring her body language. His behavior was appropriate for a seven-year-old boy. Although he was somewhat impulsive in his display, he created a very accurate characterization of the nurse. Unfortunately, the nurse overreacted, threatening the boy with severe punishment if he didn't stop making faces at her. As she escalated her threats, his mocking behavior escalated to the point where two large male staff members intervened, putting Jack in isolation and one-to-one watch for the rest of the day.

As Jack was being carried out, his behavior had escalated to the point where he did in fact look like an immensely disturbed child. He thrashed around, screaming loudly about the injustice in the way he was being treated. However, blame could also be assigned to the nurse, whose behavior had been unprofessional. It's easy to understand why a small child who is emotionally sensitive and interpersonally astute would become angry and disturbed in this situation. However, in part because of his diagnosis, the setting of an inpatient hospital, and the nurse's own disposition, the situation escalated, resulting in behavioral excesses that seemed to prove how disturbed the boy was.

As a teacher and clinical psychologist, I've found that my observations about my brother also applied to other individuals who had been given the diagnosis of ADHD. Although it is true that the students with ADHD often received the lowest grades in the courses I taught, they far surpassed their peers in their ability to engage the material in creative ways. They were often stimulated by what they were learning, but not interested in mastering it in the ways that are assessed through standard educational testing. Students with ADHD often made me think in ways I'd never considered before, and they wanted to forge their own understandings and push the limits of what was known by asking new questions, rather than settling for the accepted answers.

You have likely noted these very same gifts in your child, but you may feel steamrolled by the health care and educational systems, representatives of which insist that these very same traits are symptoms of disturbance. You may also have struggled with the fact that your child really is quite a handful. Children with this diagnosis are a lot of work, and they do act in problematic ways that disrupt others. This book will acknowledge both sides of this reality—the gift and the disruption it causes to others. It's important to keep in mind that a difference of any sort is likely to be disruptive. For example, intellectually precocious children who haven't been diagnosed with ADHD can also be disruptive in traditional educational settings, because they get bored and may act out, distracting other students. This book will show you how to understand your child's differences as a gift and help change those behaviors that hinder him.

CHANGING PROBLEMATIC BEHAVIORS

In addition to trying to provide a balance between the vision of ADHD as a gift and the difficult reality of managing your child's behavior and the system he interacts with, I will present a balance between shifting your vision and offering concrete exercises for changing problematic expressions of your child's behavior. This may seem like a contradiction. You may be thinking, "On the one hand, it seems like you're saying that my child is gifted, and on the other hand, it seems like you're telling me how to change my child." And it's true. But both of these things are needed, for many reasons.

Even though your child is gifted, the label of ADHD can have a negative impact, which can lead to problematic behaviors. For example, if your son thinks he is stupid, then he will have a hard time motivating himself in school. Similarly, if children with ADHD believe that they will fail because of their ADHD, then they will avoid trying, in order to protect their self-esteem. It is easier to say "I didn't try" than to say "I tried and failed." As a result of his differences and the challenges of being diagnosed with a disorder, your child may have adopted coping strategies like these, which are in fact problematic. This book will offer strategies for changing these unhelpful coping strategies.

Another reason your child may need to alter some behaviors is that the school system and health care system have not yet recognized your child's differences as a gift. This failure has probably led to negative interactions between your child and professionals in these fields, which may, in turn, have led to problematic behavior in your child. This is a common occurrence in school and treatment settings, where your child is likely to detect when he is being negated or undervalued and to have strong emotional reactions. He sees clearly how he is being dismissed and feels intensely hurt and humiliated by these interactions. These intense feelings, combined with impulsiveness, often lead to episodes of acting out that, when escalated by intolerant teachers and professionals, may be perceived as profoundly disturbed behavior.

When this dynamic is repeated, your child may develop coping strategies that appear to be ingrained behavioral problems. If these behaviors are changed, then others will be less likely to make negative judgments about your child, in turn causing even more disruptive behavior and continuing the pattern. Because of these tensions, this book will strike a balance between changing your vision of your child, helping you change your child's vision of himself, and offering specific exercises for changing and managing problematic behaviors.

POWERFUL OR POWERLESS

As a parent, you may feel powerless in your interactions with the educational and health care systems, but you do have an enormous amount of power to heal your child. The school and health care settings may not have conveyed this message to you, yet it's true.

You may have felt angry with these systems for conveying such disempowering messages to you. You may have heard that your child is profoundly disturbed, that his brain is dysfunctional, or that you must have done something wrong in raising him. These messages are not necessarily true and can be defeating to you and your child.

When you heard a seemingly hopeless diagnosis and the misguided notions about your child from people who were in positions of authority, you may have felt more powerless, assuming that they knew better than you about your child's condition. While you may not be a psychologist or teacher, the paradigm shift described in this book may be in line with your inner voice that told you the negative descriptions of your child just weren't right. While you may have struggled with your child yourself, perhaps you've found yourself resisting the severity of the diagnosis of ADHD, which may have felt more like an insult than a medical term.

Your own perceptions of your child's gifts may have become a "still, small voice" (1 Kings 19:12) by now as other authorities have drowned out your own, more-positive reactions to your child's exuberance, surplus of energy, and emotional sensitivity. *The Gift of ADHD* will help you reclaim your power in relation to yourself, your child, the school system, and your health care providers. It offers information to help you to connect with your own feelings that your child may not be as "bad" as some of the authority figures have implied. It will help you reconnect with your own belief in your child's abilities, strengths, and gifts.

Your own expectations for your child will be a powerful source of inspiration. So if you can trust your own positive feelings about your child's strengths, amplify those feelings, and communicate them clearly to your child, you can influence your child for the better.

CHAPTER SUMMARIES

The first four chapters will review the paradigm shift represented in the vision of this book—that ADHD is a gift. Chapter 1 will review current understandings of the diagnosis as a disorder and review a countertrend in psychology that argues that differences are not disorders. In line with this paradigm shift, chapter 2 will introduce you to the cognitive behavioral approach to transforming your child. Specific strategies for strengthening your bond to your child will be offered. Chapter 3 will suggest that this sweeping revision of this diagnostic label can also have the therapeutic effect of raising your child's self-esteem. This chapter will also review how self-esteem can be lowered by the diagnosis of ADHD and how each symptom of the disorder, such as impulsiveness, lack of motivation, and lack of attention can also be seen as resulting from lowered self-esteem, not only from the purported brain differences alleged to cause ADHD. Chapter 4 will encourage and support you in shifting both your vision and your behavior as you become an advocate, rather than apologist, for your child.

In chapters 5 through 9 we will review the specific nature of your child's gifts. In chapter 5 we will review the ways in which children who have been diagnosed with ADHD are creative. We will see, for example, how goofing off is often a necessary requirement for creativity. In chapter 6, we will review how your child may be gifted with an ecological consciousness—this means an attunement with the natural world. In chapter 7, we will review the interpersonal intuition common in children diagnosed with ADHD. In chapter 8, we will review the ways in which hyperactivity can be viewed as a surplus of energy and exuberance that can be tapped and rather than managed and minimized. In this chapter, specific strategies will be offered for channeling this energy in ways that do not disrupt others. In chapter 9, we'll discuss the ways in which ADHD children are emotionally sensitive and expressive. The balance between appreciating the gift and managing the lack of control it can bring will be addressed with specific strategies. The tenth and final chapter will review strategies for navigating both educational and mental health treatment systems.

As you can see, *The Gift of ADHD* will offer you practical suggestions and strategies that accommodate both your inner voice that has appreciated your child's differences and the one that has grown impatient with his behavior and frustrated with the knowledge that his behavior can be a problem for others.

CHAPTER 1

Difference Is Not a
Disorder or a Deficit

According to the *Diagnostic and Statistical Manual of Mental Disorders*, symptoms of ADHD include difficulty paying attention, impulsivity, and hyperactivity (American Psychiatric Association 2000). However, clinical anecdotal evidence suggests that individuals diagnosed with ADHD also tend to be particularly insightful, imaginative, and intuitive.

As a parent of a child with this diagnosis you are probably quite familiar with the symptoms it's associated with. Children with ADHD have difficulty controlling their behavior, act out in impulsive ways, disrupt classes and other students, and find it almost impossible to focus on academic tasks. Lack of concentration leads to poor discipline, impaired relationships (due to an inability to listen to others), and difficulty maintaining a routine.

Recent debates on ADHD reveal two dominant positions. One is that ADHD is a brain disorder, and the other is that individuals with this diagnosis are simply boisterous and not really different from others, but that our culture does not tolerate rambunctious children. This book takes yet a third position.

ONE OF THESE KIDS IS NOT LIKE THE OTHERS

It is true that ADHD children are noticeably different from children who have not been given this diagnosis. But calling this difference a disorder is based on an interpretation—one that has negative effects on your child.

The name of the diagnosis itself shows that medical terminology can be subjective and tends to pathologize a person. For example, children with ADHD have *hyperactivity,* which means "too much activity." Why are normal children not considered to have an "activity deficit" or "hypoactivity disorder"? To add insult to injury, ADHD children also have an "attention deficit." Again, one might ask why other children are not considered to have "hyperattention disorder" or an "overfocusing condition."

This is meant to illustrate that you should not be too discouraged by the medical description of your child's tendencies. Differences do *not* mean disorders, and it is an interpretative leap to say that they do. A difference could be just that—no better or worse, just different from others. Many people say that variety is the spice of life, but psychiatrists do not agree. They are trained to see differences as disorders. If one were to apply this logic to gender, then the medical profession might well label women with a "penis-deficit/hypermammary disorder."

The other way to think of difference is that it can be a gift, indicating that a person with that difference is in some way better than people who don't have it. In fact, the basis of evolution and natural selection is mutation, or difference. As a species, we have evolved through differences that are found to be adaptive. Many differences give people advantages. Also, in our culture, we advance in leaps and bounds through creativity—the ability to think differently from others.

In earlier times, a person's career depended on the ability to follow specific instructions given by authority figures. However, it can be argued that in today's technological culture a person is more likely to get ahead by coming up with different ways of seeing the world than by conforming to authority. With that in mind, I put forth the idea that not only is ADHD a difference, but it is also a gift. It confers advantages to the child that are not yet fully appreciated.

One way in which ADHD children are different is that they are more engaged with the organic world in a sensuous way. They may have more difficulty with abstract book knowledge, but they often appreciate nature, animals, and the human body in a direct, engaged way. These kids seem to demonstrate a form of ecological intelligence that some people have argued is necessary for saving the planet (Goleman 2009) from rampant pollution and environmental destruction. The perspective of this book is that children with ADHD have a different way of doing things that may allow them to solve problems that cannot be solved by doing things in the normal way.

A DISORDER OF THE BRAIN?

The perspective of this book is more informed by the current understanding of neuroplasticity of the brain than the current understanding of ADHD is. Neuroplasticity is a recent scientific breakthrough that shows us that the brain actually changes in response to a person's experience. In short, it tells us that we have the power to rewire our own brain. According to Daniel Siegel, "When we focus our attention in specific ways, we are activating the brain's circuitry.

This activation can strengthen the synaptic linkages in those areas" (2007, 31).

You have probably been told that ADHD is first a disorder, and second a medical dysfunction related to *brain* pathology (a dysfunction or disease of the brain). Current explanations highlight the importance of *neuropsychological* deficits (a psychological problem attributed to faulty brain functioning) and brain anomalies. Though many brain regions, such as the frontal cortex and the nucleus accumbens, have been implicated in the causing of ADHD, it remains true that "unlike illnesses such as diabetes, arthritis, or epilepsy, there is no physiological or pathological evidence for ADHD. The diagnosis is entirely subjective and is based on how we interpret a collection of symptomatic behaviors" (Shannon 2007, 229). Thus, even though the brain likely contributes to the symptoms of ADHD, a specific causal link and clear method of biological assessment have yet to be found.

If the lessons of neuroplasticity are taken to heart, we will hear children diagnosed with ADHD saying things like "My brain has a difference called ADHD. Scientists know that the brain can be changed, so I am working hard to increase my brain's capacity." This perspective increases a child's motivation. He works hard because he thinks of himself as a brain athlete; indeed, he changes his brain and goes on to lots of success. This is an example of how telling yourself, or your child, a different story can result in a different outcome. Sometimes we think of stories as misrepresenting reality (for example, a parent might say, "Oh, he's just telling stories"). But we are learning that the stories we tell can create reality. It's time for neuroplasticity to be the major theme in our ADHD stories.

Psychology and medical science tend to call any difference a disorder. So, while your doctor, psychiatrist, or psychologist may have very complicated medical explanations for your child's disorder, and studies discussed in the media may seem to provide that there are brain differences and pathology related to ADHD, you need not be fully convinced that he has actual brain pathology. There may, in fact, be significant brain differences, but these do not have to indicate brain disorders.

It's important for you and your child to be able to question the belief that the differences you see in your child are part of a medical disorder related to brain pathology and therefore unchangeable. Otherwise you create expectations that can make it more difficult for you to help yourself and your child. You *can* change his behavior and emotional impulsivity, but you and your child will need to believe that change is possible and expect to see improvements through the exercises described in this book.

Loss of Self-Esteem Due to Diagnosis

One of the reasons it is so important to understand that a difference is not a disorder is that the notion that it is a disorder may undermine your child's self-esteem. Any medical or psychological diagnosis can have this effect, but ADHD particularly so (Migden 2002). A diagnosis can become a central aspect of a person's identity. With a diagnosis that has the words "deficit" and "disorder" in it, the person may begin to see himself as simply defective. As described later in this chapter, the diagnosis may convey to your child the following messages:

- He has a disease.

- He is a victim of a disease and therefore is not in control of his behavior.

- The self is fundamentally untrustworthy because it is disordered or ill.

All of these messages can lead to low self-esteem. In fact, this sense of shaken or damaged identity can, in itself, lead to behavioral problems that look remarkably like ADHD, resulting in a vicious circle. We can see how this dynamic often plays out by reading Mike's story below.

THE LEGACY OF A DIAGNOSIS

Mike was a twenty-one-year-old student at a midwestern university. He was a psychology major but was unsure what career path he would follow. He described himself as struggling with the task of "growing up." He said that he was having difficulties acclimating to society because of repeated failure experiences in the academic arena. He had been a C student in grade school, high school, and college. He attributed his lack of success to poor habits and a lack of motivation. Since he was a child, he had been diagnosed many times with ADHD and had undergone repeated testing. He described his academic experience as an "eternal struggle." Mike thought that the fact that he had a disorder meant that it was impossible for him to succeed—that it meant that he was not talented and that everybody else had something he didn't. He even told his psychologist that the thing that made him most upset was this idea that there was something fundamentally wrong with him. He said that when he compared himself to others he believed that he was handicapped, that he couldn't even compete with or compare himself to them because his disorder meant he was worse than other people. He said his diagnosis of ADHD meant that not only did he have problems reading books but he could not succeed in school or in life. Mike thought that the diagnosis meant that he was, on the whole, a failure.

He told his therapist that he could not see why he should even try if the diagnosis meant he would never succeed. All of these negative feelings made him want to avoid his schoolwork and try to stay out of school as much as possible. Yet coming from a family of exceptional academic achievement made Mike think that he had no choice but to get a college education.

Mike's reflections suggest that his avoidance of academic pursuits was in part a result of the diagnosis. Having been told that he had a deficit disorder, he avoided the arena (academic) in which he understood himself to be flawed. His lack of interest and motivation in this arena can be attributed to what he called a "survival instinct":

Mike believed that, because he was destined to fail, he could keep his self-esteem intact by not trying. Whereas this lack of interest is typically taken to be a symptom of the disorder, in Mike's case this behavior might actually have been a symptom of the diagnosis itself. His experience also poignantly illustrates the extent to which the label affected his core sense of self. Further, his comments illustrated the idea that "diagnoses act like computer viruses, changing and erasing memories" (Hillman and Ventura 1992, 74). Additionally, psychologist James Hillman (1983, 15) has warned:

> The force of diagnostic stories cannot be exaggerated. Once one has been written into a particular clinical fantasy with its expectations, its typicalities, its character traits, and the rich vocabulary it offers for recognizing oneself, one then begins to recapitulate one's life into the shape of the story...
> A diagnosis is indeed a gnosis: a mode of self-knowledge that creates a cosmos in its image.

So, as Hillman points out, the diagnosis itself began to lower Mike's view of himself. As a result of both the diagnosis and his lowered self-esteem, he also experienced lack of motivation in school. Because he believed himself to be handicapped in the school setting, the diagnosis led to him to wonder why he should even try. This is one area that this book will help address—changing your child's thoughts about himself in order to gain improvements in his symptoms.

Mike felt flawed and hopeless in part because he had been given a diagnosis from the mental health system that told him he had a disorder. This idea that his differences constituted a flaw or disorder also came from his interactions with teachers, who are part of the educational system. Let's look at the two main culprits in our under-standing of the traits of ADHD as a disorder: the mental health system and the educational system.

THE MENTAL HEALTH SYSTEM

Although your psychologist, psychiatrist, or pediatrician may seem like an authority that you cannot challenge, many mental health providers do make a fundamental mistake.

A current trend in the mental health system is toward understanding psychological issues according to a medical model (Furman 2002). The medical model involves viewing behavioral symptoms as organic diseases that should be treated with medical interventions. The medical model presents ADHD as a brain dysfunction to be treated with medication that changes the biology of the brain.

The Problems with the Medical Model

While "medicalizing" psychological symptoms may serve insurance companies and practitioners, it may not always be in the best interest of clients. By calling a psychological disturbance a disease, mental health practitioners fail to consider the ways in which symptoms are meaningful in the context of their clients' lives (Leitner, Faidley, and Celentana 2000). For example, a child who has experienced family stressors, peer rejection, and failure at school may disrupt the classroom as an expression of anxiety and anger toward an environment that he perceives as punishing. In this way, the symptom of disruptive behavior can be seen as meaningful from the child's perspective rather than as a symptom of a medical disease.

SUBJECTIVE ASSESSMENT

Another significant problem with the medical model is that it misrepresents the process of diagnosis, which is necessarily subjective. Because the symptoms themselves are behaviors rather than biological symptoms, such as fever, the assessment of the disturbance is essentially a social judgment. In short, if a teacher is telling you that your child's behavior is unmanageable, there is no thermometer that can confirm the teacher's judgment in an objective sense. As a social judgment, the assessment is naturally biased, because the person making the judgment and the social setting in which the behavior occurs are not objective. In other words, the person making the judgment may be biased, and there may also be a real problem in the social setting that your child is responding to. For example, recall Jack's story, where the young boy was responding to a setting that was harshly judgmental and lacking in caring or support for him in his predicament. His behavior became out of control in response to the punitive actions of a care provider. So when psychologists provide a label that carries the weight of a medical diagnosis, they are in some ways making the mistake of transferring medical notions, which are more objective, to the psychological and behavioral realm, which can be measured only in subjective and biased ways by individuals in particular settings.

> Telling a child that ADHD is a medical disorder sets up a profound barrier to treating the symptoms and helping your child heal.

UNDERMINING TREATMENT POSSIBILITIES

The medical model for understanding ADHD presents a lot of problems when it comes to treatment. The diagnosis itself, which conveys an irrefutable medical diagnosis rooted in brain pathology, seems to contradict the idea that the symptoms could be reduced. But, unlike more stable medical diagnoses, the realms of behavior and emotion are actually considerably affected by how much you and your child believe that he can change his behavior. The more you believe, the more success you will have in effecting the changes you and your child want to make.

Telling a child that ADHD is a medical disorder sets up a profound barrier to treating the symptoms and helping your child heal.

Because behavior and emotions are shaped so powerfully by expectations and because the label of ADHD sets up strong expectations, the label itself can be damaging and get in the way of effective treatment. Why is this true? If a doctor tells a child that he has a deficit, then you can expect that the child will take the doctor's statement as unimpeachable truth and come to understand himself as flawed. He will likely act out in ways that reflect diminished self-esteem and reduce his chances of positive treatment results.

The label also affects how other people see and treat your child, setting up negative expectations that get in the way of positive treatment. If a teacher is told that your child has ADHD, that teacher may act toward your child in ways that convey the expectation that your child will be difficult to manage. An enormous body of information has shown us that teachers' expectations for students are very powerful in determining the subsequent performance of those students. In one of the most well-known studies, teachers were told that a certain group of students were very gifted and that another group of students were average. The expectations given to the teachers did not actually reflect the abilities of the students at all. The researchers found that the students who were expected to do very well had made substantial improvements by the end of the year, whereas those for whom the teachers had lower expectations did not make substantial improvements (see Rosenthal 1987 for a review of studies). These studies demonstrate that teachers' expectations of students are a self-fulfilling prophecy—children have a tendency to perform in ways that are consistent with teachers' expectations for them. Because research has shown that diagnoses of ADHD are increasingly suggested by teachers (Sax and Kautz 2003), their expectations must be increasingly influencing children's access to or admission into the mental health system.

> Because behavior and emotions are shaped so powerfully by expectations and because the label of ADHD sets up strong expectations, the label itself can be damaging and get in the way of effective treatment.

As mentioned above, once the child is admitted into the mental health system, the diagnosis can interfere with the most potent treatments for changing behavior. In a medical setting, if the cure for a fever is aspirin, then the aspirin will work no matter what the doctor tells you about the nature of your disorder. However, in psychological settings, the very work of therapy and healing your child is often obstructed by the diagnosis. For example, all cognitive therapies for psychological disorders involve changing the way clients think about themselves. If a child feels that it is hopeless for him to even try in school, a cognitive therapy will help your child to challenge these thoughts of hopelessness. Unfortunately, the diagnosis of ADHD tends to undermine the power of these therapeutic interventions. The diagnosis seems to say to the child, "You have a disorder that makes you inalterably less than other students." This message has negative effects on your child's thoughts about himself and his abilities and can undermine otherwise-powerful cognitive therapies.

The diagnosis also seems to convey that ADHD is the same in every situation and is immune to change without medical interventions. This is not a fair way of representing a psychological and behavioral difference, because your child's symptoms will vary according to setting and interaction with specific individuals. You have likely noticed this yourself. Around certain people or in specific settings your child may act like an angel, and in other settings the telltale behavioral symptoms emerge with intensity. This means that, unlike a medical disorder, your child's differences are responsive to individuals and environments—they can be dramatically affected by changing situations and by guidance on how to respond to challenging situations. In summary, the fact that the constellation of behaviors labeled ADHD is considered a medical disorder conveys the expectation to parents, children, and teachers that behavior should be unchanging, constant, and made better only by medicine. In many ways, the diagnosis creates an expectation that manifests in the very symptoms it sets out to describe.

THE PROBLEM WITH PSYCHOLOGISTS AND PSYCHIATRISTS

Psychologists and psychiatrists are trained in the categorization of pathology and disorders. Training for diagnosing disorders focuses on asking the question "Which diagnosis fits?" rather than "Is there an alternative to a clinical label?" Many children will have many of the symptoms of ADHD some of the time. The problem is that too often these children will end up with a diagnosis of ADHD when in fact they simply have an active, flexible, highly aroused temperament and not a mental disorder. A child who can be challenging to deal with is not the same thing as a child with a mental disorder.

In her book *When the Labels Don't Fit* (2008) Barbara Probst guides parents through the many different personality types, temperaments, and learning styles that look a lot like ADHD. She describes several predictable personality traits that map onto ADHD, such as high arousal, broad focus, high intensity, irregularity and unpredictability, quick tempo, nonperfectionism, and flexible and divergent thinking. This list of personality traits looks a lot like the symptom checklist psychologists use to make a diagnosis of ADHD. As mentioned in the preface, a child should only receive a diagnosis of ADHD if a serious impairment in functioning can be documented in more than one setting. Knowing that the diagnosis itself has possible consequences for your child, you will want to ensure that a thorough evaluation has been completed before you settle on the diagnosis.

THE EDUCATIONAL SYSTEM

A defining feature of the U.S. public educational system is that it reflects the lack of value our culture assigns to those who educate our children. Current educational systems are plagued by insufficient resources, resulting in overcrowded classes, overburdened teachers, and inadequate support from school psychologists or social workers (Furman 2002). Given these challenges, the medical model of dealing with ADHD provides the quickest fix. Providing medication to control children's behavior is easier and cheaper than developing schools that can respond to the individual needs of students.

As you'll recall, when my brother was given his diagnosis, my mother found that he could go without any medications in certain school years, depending on the teacher. Perhaps the diagnosis of

ADHD did not carry as much baggage then as it does today, and teachers were free to respond to my brother as a unique individual rather than as a troubled child. Or maybe many teachers did not even know what the diagnosis meant or were not aware that he had been given this diagnosis. Today, these diagnoses follow the child from year to year, and of course every teacher knows precisely what to expect from a child given this diagnosis.

Because of this recent trend, any child who has a different learning style is most likely walking into the classroom, even in a new year with a new teacher, with a heavy load of expectations that are not in his favor. It's not surprising that his symptoms seem so consistent from year to year, from teacher to teacher, if you consider that he's walking into the same set of expectations.

While the mental health field has determined that your child has a deficit disorder, research has shown that children diagnosed with ADHD, on average, do not have lower IQ scores than other children (Psychological Corporation 1997). The only significant deficits are in working memory, which means that they cannot hold numbers or other information in their memory as long as other children. Of course, a deficit in working memory doesn't mean your child cannot succeed in the classroom. Research has shown that 50 to 75 percent of a child's academic success is dependent on nonintellectual factors such as persistence, psychological health, and curiosity (Groth-Marnat 2003). This means that your child has a great deal of potential for succeeding in school, though teachers in traditional school settings may tend to view ADHD as a disadvantage. This book will show you that one of the gifts of ADHD is your child's enormous curiosity and energy. In addition, throughout this book you will be provided with exercises for increasing your child's persistence and personal adjustment. All of these will help your child succeed in school.

Handling Difference

Children with ADHD are immensely curious and interested but learn best through engaging their senses and through immersion in the organic world. If every day were a field trip, these kids would be considered geniuses. They learn by doing, by being active, by being engaged with the objects of their curiosity.

Recent advances in psychology and education reveal that there are many different types of intelligence and that each child has a unique profile of strengths and weaknesses. Unfortunately, the education system is not set up to handle these kinds of differences in learning styles. As it stands, the current school model focuses almost exclusively on developing one or two types of intelligence—abstract reasoning in verbal and mathematical realms and the acquisition of abstract facts and knowledge. Many children, even traditionally gifted children, are failed by the excessive focus on the development of abstract reasoning and learning through book knowledge. ADHD children are particularly failed by this system because they tend not to learn well in the ways that schools typically teach.

The school may develop an individualized education plan (IEP) for your child, usually at your request, but this plan probably won't in any significant way accommodate the true gifts and differences of your child. Unfortunately, the educational system has profoundly limited resources and as a result often fails children with significant differences. Unable to recognize the lack of flexibility of the educational system to accommodate these differences, its representatives (the teachers and administrators) may blame the child for not having a mind that fits its model. I don't mean to say that your child's teachers are bad people or that they are trying to hurt your child; it's just that the system is flawed and tends to work only for certain kinds of kids.

As is the case with the mental health system, this tendency for the educational system to point the finger at your child rather than acknowledging its own failings further exacerbates your child's problems. Rather than hearing "You are different, and our system is not set up to meet your needs," your child gets the message "Because you don't fit our system, you must have a disorder."

I review these failings not to make you feel hopeless but rather to empower you in becoming an advocate for your child. In my experience, individual teachers and mental health care professionals are caring people who want to help each child. As a parent working one-on-one with your child's teacher, you have enormous power to engage the individuals who work closely with your child. You can help to change their vision and expectations. You will learn more about advocating for your child later in the book.

> The perspective of this book is that, whether you choose medication or not, finding and focusing on your child's gifts will be an important way to encourage positive change in your child.

THE MEDICATION DEBATE

Both the educational system and the mental health system rely on the use of medication to suppress the symptoms of ADHD. Ritalin, the most popular of these medications, is the brand name for methylphenidate, which belongs to a classification of mood-altering drugs that stimulate brain functioning (psychostimulants). Although the prescription for medication is so commonplace that most parents and teachers have stopped questioning its use, a great debate continues regarding using medication to treat ADHD.

Given the theory that ADHD is a brain disorder, it makes sense that a drug that alters brain functioning would be the cure. Nevertheless, as a parent, you will likely find the decision about whether or not to use medication to be a difficult one, leaving you with nagging doubts no matter which choice you make. The perspective of this book is that, whether you choose medication or not, finding and focusing on your child's gifts will be an important way to encourage positive change in your child. So the information offered herein is entirely separate from the question of medication. For informational purposes, let's briefly examine both sides of the argument about the use of medications.

Medication as the Answer

The main argument for the use of medications like Ritalin to treat ADHD is that these medications work. Simply put, they decrease the symptoms of ADHD. Children who are on Ritalin can sit still longer, can focus more, and display fewer problematic behaviors. The largest-scale study comparing medication to behavioral interventions found that—in the short term—children showed more improvements in ADHD symptoms if they were receiving medication than they did if they were receiving only behavioral treatments (MTA Cooperative Group 1999).

In this way, medication may allow your child to manage his behavior and therefore to hit appropriate developmental milestones on time. Medication enables immediate, positive effects, to the benefit of the child, parents, and teachers. Parents and teachers are relieved of the constant stress of managing a child who, without medication, seems incapable of managing himself.

Why Medications May Not Be the Answer

There are many problems with using medications to treat ADHD. The first and foremost of these problems is that the largest, most rigorously conducted scientific research (MTA Study Group 2009) shows that, after eight years of follow-up, the benefits are not observed for those who initially received medication treatment compared to those in other conditions. The long-term benefits are not easily found, and there is reason for concern about the short-term and long-term negative effects of being treated with ADHD medications. Short-term negative effects may include insomnia, stomach problems, irritability, headaches, and heart palpitations. Long-term effects are unknown, but neuropsychologists argue, based on knowledge of those who are addicted to nonprescription stimulants and of recent animal studies, that "stimulants could alter the structure and function of the brain in ways that may depress mood, boost anxiety and, in sharp contrast to their short-term effects, lead to cognitive deficits" (Higgens 2009, 40).

Another concern regarding longer-term side effects is the potential for addiction to these drugs. According to one leader in the field, "People abuse prescription stimulants for various reasons—to get high, to improve academic or athletic performance, or to lose weight—putting themselves at risk for dangerous health consequences. Young people are at particular risk—in 2005, 8.6 percent and 4.4 percent of twelfth graders reported past-year non-medical use of amphetamine and methylphenidate, respectively" (Volkow 2006).

A deeper concern has to do with the support that the child will not get because the medication will treat the symptoms but not underlying causes. It's possible that the symptoms are in part being caused by issues such as a loss in the family, high levels of family stress, and mental and physical health problems in parents or siblings. Children are very sensitive and their behavior can easily be affected by anxiety and loss. By suppressing the symptoms with medications, the underlying issues for the child may never get addressed and can show up in more disruptive forms later in life.

To Medicate or Not to Medicate

As a parent, you will have to make your own decision, in collaboration with your child's psychiatrist, taking into consideration the costs and benefits of medicating your child. If your child is currently on medication and you are interested in taking your child off the drugs, you might wish to consult an important resource, *Your Drug May Be Your Problem: How and Why to Stop Taking Psychiatric Medications*, by Peter Breggin with David Cohen (1999).

SUPPORTING YOUR CHILD

One thing researchers have determined about treating people with behavioral and emotional disorders is that the relationship to the client is one of the most powerful factors in helping that person change. The same concept applies to your relationship with your child. So, in order for you to help your child, you must have a supportive relationship with him. Many times, a child's problematic behaviors cause frustration in parents, making them antagonistic toward their child. This reaction is understandable, because children with ADHD do require an enormous amount of energy and attention, and their behavior can test a parent's limits in many ways. Also, because of the pressures from educators and health care professionals, parents may feel compelled to apologize for their child's behavior, which amounts to an admission that the child is in the wrong, rather than defending the child or pointing out his strengths.

The more frustrated you become with your child, the more he will feel hurt and act out in ways that cause problems for himself and others. The more you can see your child's difference as a gift rather than a disorder, the stronger your relationship will be and the more helpful you can be. Further, because your child may interpret the diagnosis as invalidating, he may believe that you buy into the view that he is defective and assume that you lack confidence in him. In order for you to use the tools in this book most effectively, you need to find ways to make your child feel that you are on his side and that you think very highly of him. Your relationship with your child will be a powerful agent for transformation.

Accept Who Your Child Is, but Set Limits

The best way to forge a strong and supportive relationship with your child is to achieve a balance: giving him the strong validation that he needs while at the same time communicating to him the changes that need to be made. Although this seems contradictory, it will make sense to your child. Because your child needs to feel safe, strong, and confident to engage the world, he will need lots of acceptance and validation just for being who he is. This book will help you give him that, because it will guide you in reframing his negative labels as positive qualities—affirmation that your child deeply needs to receive.

In addition to needing affirmation, your developing child also needs the support, direction, and guidance of his parents. He may not communicate this to you directly, but it is a fundamental need of any child to receive direction and feedback. At heart, children recognize that they would be in trouble if they ruled the world. In fact, many behavioral disturbances are actually efforts to engage parents in setting limits. Children get very anxious if they have too much power and need reassurance that their parents are strong and will set limits when needed. Your child may communicate exactly the opposite to you and tell you to leave him alone, but inside he is crying out for direction and compassionate guidance. Your child will respond positively to your efforts to change his behavior if you set strong boundaries while communicating a feeling of love for who he is.

Reading this book will help you achieve this delicate balance. Because the foundation of the book is the concept of reframing ADHD as a gift, you can use the awareness and cognitive exercises offered here to communicate to your child that you love and accept the very traits that others are calling problems. The behavioral strategies will also help you to communicate to your child that you care so much about him that you will play an active role in guiding his behavior and that you will be willing to set limits when needed. For instance, exercises will guide you and your child to understand that the symptom of hyperactivity can also be understood as an abundance of energy. In this way, you are validating the child. In addition, you will learn to help your child become aware of ways in which his expression of this energy becomes distracting to others in school settings. Further, you'll learn techniques for shaping your child's behavior in ways that reduce the frequency of these distracting behaviors.

Believe That Change Is Possible

Another reason for you to counteract the effects of the label ADHD is that, in order for your child to make changes, he needs to believe that change is possible. The impression that ADHD is like a medical disease may make it seem to you and your child that it is not possible to make internal changes that would turn things around. However, ADHD is not like a medical disease, in that it is not something a child "has" but a set of behaviors the child does. For this reason, it is important that, if your child has been given this diagnosis, you, as a parent, provide balance by reframing the disorder as a difference and assuring your child that he can change his behavior.

Increase Motivation to Change

Another way in which reframing the diagnosis of ADHD will help you and your child is it will increase your and your child's motivation to change. Experts in the field of psychology have recently begun to acknowledge that clients have different levels of readiness to change. Interventions may be offered to clients with the assumption that they are highly motivated to make changes in their lives, but many clients are resistant to change, for many reasons. With ADHD, you and your child may not be motivated to work at the exercises, because you feel hopeless. Why exert so much effort to change, you might wonder, when your doctor has told you that it is a brain disorder and that the only treatment is a medication that changes the brain chemistry? Isn't it easier to take pills than to work hard to change behaviors and emotions?

In order for you to feel motivated to change and to increase your child's motivation to change, you have to believe that your hard work will pay off. By reframing the disorder as gift, understanding the significant resources your child has, and conveying this positive message to your child, you can increase motivation to make changes. Many of the strategies and exercises you'll learn in this book will require a commitment of time and energy from you and your child. In order to follow through you will need motivation and an expectation that this investment will yield benefits for both you and your child. But if you understand the nature of your child's gifts, you will likely have more hope for your child and therefore feel more engaged and willing to do the hard work of helping him change.

You can also increase your own motivation to practice the exercises by viewing them as a chance for you to reconnect with your child. You may want to reframe the exercises as a guided "play time" with your child. You can set up a consistent, special time to do them, and you and your child can engage in them together in the spirit of fun. The exercises are designed to be appealing to children and to use images that evoke fun and play. For example, in chapter 9, when we discuss managing emotions, you will find an exercise that involves surfing the waves of emotion. Thus, the exercises show your child how managing and connecting with his own experience can also be fun and playful. If you take such an attitude and let yourself play with your child in these exercises, you can serve as a powerful model for your child.

Put Your Child in Control of ADHD

The diagnosis may seem to carry the subtle message that your child is a victim of a disorder and that he is therefore less capable of making choices. Sometimes parents or children think that, because ADHD is a disorder that they passively suffer from, the kids are not in control of and therefore are not responsible for their behavior. In the face of this assumption, they are more likely to act out in impulsive and irresponsible ways (in other words, "My ADHD made me do it").

The diagnosis of ADHD also serves as a barrier to healing because it conveys to you and your child that he cannot rely on his own judgment. The pathway to healing from ADHD includes a gain in self-esteem so he can trust himself to make important life choices and commitments. For example, children with ADHD often have an uncanny ability to read others. Often, because they express these insights in seemingly irreverent ways, they are punished for the expression of this gift, leading them to doubt their own perceptions. This leads to conflict and confusion and lowered self-esteem, which themselves lead to disturbances in the children's relationships with others. In this way, the children's inability to trust their own experience of the world—again, in part a consequence of the diagnosis—leads to some of the very symptoms the diagnosis points to.

The key to changing your child's behavior is for you to recognize that your child *can* control some of his problematic behaviors. This book will help you to help your child reclaim control and recognize his own power over his thoughts, feelings, and behaviors.

SUMMARY

As a parent of a child with ADHD, you've got your work cut out for you. You probably struggle with your own feelings of hopelessness about changing your child. You struggle with your child's motivation, or lack of motivation, to change. Mental health and educational systems may seem overly eager to change your child in ways you might question. Although managing the complex puzzle of parenting a child with ADHD may seem overwhelming, the goal of reclaiming and celebrating your child's gifts is worth it.

You have the power to delight in your child's differences and gifts and to share that delight with your child, your child's teachers, and other significant individuals in your child's life. Most important, through your supportive and validating relationship with your child, you will reconnect with him and have the relationship with him that you truly want. This relationship in itself will be the most powerful healing agent of all.

CHAPTER 2

How You Can Transform Your Child

One of the leading methods of therapy for treating a wide range of psychological and behavioral problems is called cognitive behavioral therapy (CBT). This type of therapy focuses on changing thoughts and behaviors that create symptoms.

COGNITIVE BEHAVIORAL THERAPY

One of the central assumptions of the cognitive behavioral approach offered in this book is that thoughts cause feelings and behaviors. Therefore, changing or challenging your child's self-defeating thoughts can help her manage feelings and behaviors. Additionally, changing her behaviors can affect her thoughts and feelings.

A cognitive behavioral therapist will actively work to challenge irrational and unproductive thoughts and attitudes, helping the client change these to attitudes and beliefs that will lead to more productive behaviors. Sometimes therapists will ask clients to directly change behaviors and observe changes in the thoughts and feelings that follow.

Throughout this book, you will be offered many different exercises and strategies for helping your child identify and challenge thoughts that lead to disruptive behaviors. The cognitive behavioral approach also relies on breaking big behavior changes into very small and manageable tasks. This helps increase motivation because it does not require sweeping, permanent changes all at once. Instead, by identifying and meeting small challenges, your child will have success earlier and more consistently, which will further increase motivation to keep making changes.

YOUR POWER TO ASSIST IN CHANGE

As a parent, you have the power to identify and shape your child's attitudes and behaviors. This book will provide you with a rich resource and specific strategies, techniques, and playful exercises for helping your child adopt the most positive thoughts and attitudes. The easiest way to get your child to sign on to a healing program is to captivate her interest by making it a game. Many of the exercises can be framed as games and can go a long way toward breaking the vicious circle that can make your child's differences seem like a disorder. When you cast the exercises as pretend games, your child cannot fail—it's a game, so these exercises are less likely to backfire and make your child more discouraged if she doesn't fully follow through. Similarly, if the exercises are cast as experiments in which the point is to find out how this new attitude or thought affects the child's experience, she cannot fail.

One of the challenges of treating symptoms of ADHD is to engage and motivate kids who have trouble paying attention or following through. After all, if the child could follow the treatment program, she would probably have an easier time following behavior expectations in most situations and would not be exhibiting problematic symptoms. For this reason, treatment programs or self-help programs that rely on self-discipline from the child are likely to fail. This program of change has been designed to channel your child's high level of energy, curiosity, and areas of interest to help her want to engage.

Strengthen the Bond with Your Child

Though this program will not demand of your child skills that she doesn't have, it will demand a commitment from you as the parent. However, you will find that the playful nature of the exercises will serve to strengthen your bond and relationship with your child. This is not an extra chore—it is part of your existing commitment to spend more time with your child and to enrich your relationship.

Sometimes parents are hesitant to implement suggestions from self-help books or mental health practitioners because they feel that the suggestions might pit them against their own child or add to the burden of parenting rather than increase the joy. The exercises in this book will help to increase your intimacy with your child and, because they are validating for your child and cast as play, will not pit your will against your child's or involve getting her to adhere to a demanding program for reform. The exercises in this book may not only help your child with the specific problem of ADHD but also address the overall problem of how to spend positive time with your child.

Reframe

Looking at ADHD as a gift will help you to increase your child's motivation by offering praise for the very symptoms that others have found so problematic. Reframing the diagnosis is an example of a central cognitive behavioral technique for treating any disorder: reframing. In reframing, you change your cognitive interpretation of some trait about yourself or some event in the real world that has upset you. For example, if you find out that someone you are close to did not tell you about something major that was happening in his or her life, you might get upset and think he or she is trying to keep secrets from you. If you reframe this situation, you might consider that maybe this person did not tell you what was going on because he or she wanted to protect you from getting upset. As you can probably imagine, the emotions and behavior that follow these different interpretations will be quite different.

The strategy of finding alternative interpretations of events and characteristics of the self is a central method of change in cognitive behavioral therapy, the approach used in this book. Helping your child to reframe the diagnosis of ADHD as a gift that makes her different from others in potentially positive ways is central to her healing process. Not only will the reframing help as a strategy in and of itself, but it will also provide the motivation for engaging in the program of change offered in this book.

Increase Motivation to Change

As mentioned in chapter 1, a reason many treatments fail is that the therapist or program of change operates under the assumption that the person who needs help is motivated and ready to change. Often the person is not, and then therapists may blame their clients for not wanting to change, or individuals may heap more blame on themselves for their failure to follow through on rigorous programs. Understanding ADHD as a gift will get around this problem in two main ways: first, you are increasing motivation by elevating your child's self-esteem; second, you are validating your child by conveying the message that she is fundamentally okay just being who she is. You are not trying to eliminate a disorder; you are trying to shape your child so that she can use these differences in ways that help her meet her goals.

The most important thing is to cast this program so that it isn't about changing who your child is but rather helps her achieve the goals that she really wants to achieve. In this way, you are not working against your child but are offering your time and energy to help her get what she wants. Children with ADHD want to be liked by their peers and teachers, and they want to excel and be respected for their abilities, but they have a hard time doing these things without help. Before you begin this program, you might want to warm up with some of the following exercises, which will help your child to overcome negative expectations.

EXERCISES FOR SPECIFIC CHALLENGES

The rest of the chapter will be devoted to exercises for addressing specific symptoms of ADHD. You may want to read through all the exercises first and then use the ones that you and your child will feel most comfortable with. There are many exercises throughout the book, and it's important that you find a handful of exercises that you and your child really enjoy and that don't feel like chores. If your child doesn't like some of the games, you don't have to push it. Try some of the others to find some that she really likes, and repeat those.

If you and she can engage in some of the exercises regularly, you can expect to see your child (and your relationship with her) transform. The exercises are designed to tap your child's existing interests and strengths, so present them to your child as fun games rather than as a reform strategy. To make them easier to implement, try to find creative ways to integrate these games into your lives. For example, some of the pretend games can be played while driving in the car or sitting in a waiting room.

The Challenge of Persistence

One of the most often documented differences between children diagnosed with ADHD and other children is that ADHD children do not persist as long as other children do in academic tasks. Studies have found that ADHD children who are asked to solve cognitive puzzles will have less success and will quit working more often than others (Hoza et al. 2001). In addition, observers noted children with ADHD putting forth less effort and being less cooperative than those in a control group (ibid.).

The following exercise will help address the causes of this characterization of children diagnosed with ADHD. A typical strategy in cognitive behavioral therapy involves the therapist asking the client to evaluate the costs and benefits of a particular thought, belief, or attitude. The exercise that follows invites your child to imagine the long-term consequences of a belief that she does not need to work hard.

EXERCISE: Why Try?

When your child says, "Why try?" or makes similar comments, you can offer many different helpful responses. Try the following exercise with your child the next time she expresses this sort of dysfunctional attitude in response to challenges. This exercise will demonstrate to your child the power of this thought and how it can lead to self-defeating behaviors.

Ask your child to imagine her favorite cartoon, movie, or book character, and ask her how that character's life would be different if that character adopted a "why try?" attitude.

The more concrete you can make this exercise, the better. For example, after watching a specific episode of a cartoon or on the way home from a movie, ask your child what would have happened differently in that story if the character had said, "Why try?"

In this way, your child can begin to understand the power of thoughts over her own life and success or failure. By looking at how a thought can affect fictional characters, your child can explore this powerful principle from a more objective point of view, which is less threatening than thinking directly about her own attitudes.

RESPECTING AND UTILIZING YOUR CHILD'S SPECIALIZED INTERESTS TO INCREASE MOTIVATION

Children with ADHD think organically and imaginally. They may struggle with abstract reasoning that is removed from everyday life and their interests, but they are often ardently curious and have passions in specific areas of specialization. The good news is that they can be highly motivated if you engage these areas of intense interest.

The tricky part about cognitive interventions is that, on one hand, you want to change your child's thoughts and behavior, and, on the other hand, children with ADHD are in deep need of validation and acceptance. For this reason, one strategy for teaching some of the basic principles is to start out with fictional characters that your child already has an intense interest in. As in the preceding exercise, because you are talking about a character, rather than the child herself, she will be less likely to feel invalidated and become defensive and antagonistic.

As a rule, you will want to work with your child's passionate interests. Children with ADHD often channel much of their energy and enthusiasm toward what seems like a waste of time to adults. They may get very excited about sports figures, sports teams, animals, dinosaurs, or subject areas that don't seem likely to lead to academic success. But these areas of intense interest are actually tremendous resources for you as you go about supporting and teaching your child. For example, if your child loves figure skating and identifies Sarah Hughes as a hero, then you can use that energy and channel it toward concrete behavioral change. At times when your child gets discouraged about school and says things like "I'm not good enough because I have ADHD," you can ask her to think through what Sarah Hughes's life would be like if she had said "Why try?"

One example of this strategy can be seen in the experience of a seven-year-old boy who was obsessed with knights. He talked about knights in shining armor, he drew pictures of knights, and he loved to read stories and see movies that involved knights. In this case, both the teachers and the parents were worried about this preoccupation and wondered if, in itself, it might represent a separate problem—some form of childhood obsessive-compulsive disorder, perhaps. However, all children, particularly children with ADHD, are quite imaginative and intense in their interests. Rather than communicating their anxiety about his preoccupation to the child, his parents channeled his energy around the subject of knights into an exercise to help increase motivation.

EXERCISE: The Knights

In the example above, the parents invited their son to play a game exploring the outcomes of two different knights, Sir Try-a-Lot and Sir Why-Try. (For older children, you might want to choose sports heroes rather than fictional characters. For example, you might use Lance Armstrong, the cyclist who has repeatedly won the Tour de France after recovering from cancer.)

To try this exercise, set up a fictional scenario, or ask your child to provide the details of the challenges to be overcome, perhaps including a dragon guarding a treasure or a damsel in distress. Embellish your story to draw as many parallels as possible to your child's own language and attitudes around ADHD. For example, you might say that both knights had been told by the king that, because they had a handicap, they could not be a part of the round table, and so each knight set out to find adventures on his own. One of the knights keeps trying as hard as possible in the face of challenges and the other just gives up and says, "Why try?" As you invite your child to elaborate on the fortunes of these two different knights, highlight the major themes for your child. These themes will include the power of a positive attitude to achieve goals and how our thoughts create our behavior.

Encourage your child to identify thoughts leading to emotions that might make a character say "Why try?" Help him see the connection between these thoughts, emotions, and the behaviors they encourage. Then challenge him to generate ideas or thoughts that would help the characters to overcome their challenges or to achieve their goals. If a knight was banished from the round table for having a handicap and everyone thought he wasn't as capable as the other knights, what might he say to himself in order to become a hero? Ask your child to write down examples of helpful things this character could say to himself. Help your child if he is struggling. For example, you might suggest that the knight says, "Well, I can do whatever those other knights can do—I just have to try harder." In this way, the diagnosis of ADHD can be seen as an impetus for more effort rather than an incentive to give up in frustration.

Let your child's imagination run wild as he explores the different fates of the two knights (or other characters of interest). Then you can gently bring him back to applying these principles to his own life. You might quietly remind him, for example, how this situation would apply to his struggles in social studies class, where your child feels the teacher is always "dissing" him.

Be careful to extend this period of application only as long as your child will tolerate. When he shows signs of distress, boredom, or the typical symptoms of hyperactivity, let him guide the conversation back to the imaginal arena or whatever is of more interest to him. If you push too hard, he will come to resent these games and will become bored by them. In trying to help your child heal from his difficulty paying attention, you must validate and cater to the very symptoms you are trying to help him overcome. So don't resist his lack of attention. You can maintain his attention by returning as often as necessary to his area of intense interest, be it knights, sports, or something else, and embedding the exercises within these contexts. You may also want to play the game over and over again in different settings and situations rather than drawing it out over long periods of time.

EXERCISE: Be Your Hero

You can increase the effectiveness of the preceding technique by challenging your child to a pretend game. For example, you might say, "This next week, when you feel that Ms. Wyatt is dissing you, try thinking like the knight who was banished from the round table, and try even harder in class!" Tell your child it's a game to play just for one week, or frame it as an experiment to see what effect it has on the teacher. In this way, you can attract your child's interest. Each day, remind your child about your pretend game and then follow up after school on what happened in the game.

Start out by focusing on one problem area. For example, focus on one teacher whose class is particularly distressing for your child. This way, she is likely to be able to follow through and meet with some early successes. If you were to start by suggesting that she be the knight in all her classes, or for a longer period than one week, your child may not be able to sustain the exertion required to make such a sweeping change and could give up in frustration. By starting out in one class for one week, she may be highly motivated to follow through and won't feel overwhelmed by the prospect of dramatically changing her behavior overnight.

The Challenge of Encouraging Rational Thinking

Children with ADHD need support in challenging their negative thinking. The following activities will also help build your child's executive functioning skills by increasing his ability to identify and weigh the pros and cons of any behavior.

Your child learns through being engaged with the world, by touching, tasting, feeling, and being actively immersed in what she is trying to learn. This is important to keep in mind when deciding how you will engage her in this healing program. Your child will have a very low tolerance for lectures or moralizing, as she has difficulty with (and little interest in) wading through abstract information. This means that separating facts and figures from their real-world context is almost intolerably boring for your child. The following exercise illustrates how you can use concrete, sensory objects to impress upon your child the principles of cognitive behavioral therapy.

ENGAGE YOUR CHILD'S SENSES TO INTRODUCE CBT

In the following exercise, you will help your child see that attitudes that lead to low persistence are obviously unproductive. In addition to making the process of examining her thought processes more concrete, the following exercises will serve to increase your child's commitment to this program of transformation. The more clearly your child is able to see how her thought patterns are self-defeating, the more she will be willing to engage in the other exercises.

EXERCISE: The Balance

1. Obtain a two-sided scale or balance that allows you to put objects on both sides to see which side is heavier. You will be able to use this scale for many exercises described in this book, helping your child evaluate the costs and benefits of her thoughts, beliefs, attitudes, or behaviors. If you cannot find a scale, you can do this exercise by drawing a teeter-totter on a piece of paper, writing the costs on one side and the benefits on the other, and asking your child to identify which list would be heavier. For an older child, you could ask her to draw a picture of a scale with lines below each side so she can write the costs and benefits. Also, gather a bunch of pennies to work with.

2. Sit down with your child and the scale (or the drawing of a scale or teeter-totter). Work with her to identify one of her

self-defeating thoughts, like "Why should I try if I have a deficit disorder?" You might do this by asking her what she was thinking about herself just before she engaged in a recent distracted or frustrated behavior.

3. Invite your child to evaluate the costs and benefits of the thought or belief by asking her to think of all the reasons that her belief is good for her. Designate one side of the scale as the side that weighs the benefits of this belief.

   Identify the other side of the scale as the side that you'll use to weigh the costs of the belief, or the ways in which the belief is hurtful to the child. Then encourage her to come up with some of these ways. Start with how the belief is helpful, as she will likely have more energy around that, and this will allow you to keep her attention and gain momentum for the game. Place a penny on the appropriate side of the scale for each reason your child gives. For example, she might say that this belief prevents her from trying and failing and getting hurt. If she's struggling for ideas and hasn't hit on this one, help her by suggesting that perhaps the belief prevents her from getting hurt.

   After you have completed the positive side, you can then say, "Okay, let's put a penny on the other side of the scale for each of the reasons that this belief will hurt you. What can you think of?" Your child might suggest, "When I say 'Why try?' to myself, I don't work very hard, and I don't do very well." She might say that the belief makes her feel hopeless. She might say that she doesn't get good grades in school because of this belief. On this side, encourage her and give as many hints and suggestions as possible, making this a very long list of concrete results. The idea is to generate examples of how this thought leads to negative emotions and negative behaviors, which cause her to do poorly in school.

4. Finally, show your child how the side with the costs is so much heavier than the benefits side. You may want to briefly but

explicitly make a connection to how this disparity in weight might cause her to want to change the belief. But keep in mind that she won't be able to tolerate the "moral of the story" for very long.

You will generally have more success with these exercises if you follow these guidelines:

- Keep the game embedded in the play aspect and avoid abstract moralizing.

- Do the exercises frequently and apply them to many different situations, because your child does not generalize very easily.

- Refer to your child's thoughts as "what you say to yourself." Be prepared for your child to have some difficulty identifying her thoughts and attitudes, because you are asking her to draw abstract conclusions from her immediate experience.

One important reason that your child has such a low tolerance for a lot of talk about the moral of the story is that all moralizing implies that she is wrong or something she is doing is wrong. This sounds to her like invalidation. Kids with ADHD are particularly sensitive and intuitive in regard to the underlying messages of interpersonal interactions, which tends to give them a low threshold for invalidation. For them, it is like the world's volume has been turned up to an unbearably high level and any implied, subtle, or well-meaning efforts to reform your child will be heard by her as stinging condemnation. Also bear in mind that the diagnosis of ADHD itself can be a profound invalidation of her way of being in the world. And consider that any person, and certainly any sensitive child, can only take so much invalidation.

For this reason, you will have more success with your child if you engage her senses in using the exercises in this book and work to increase her own motivation to change rather than imposing it on her in a moralizing way. There are many strategies you can use and activities you can do to make your child's desire to change come from within, rather than from a wish to please you, her teachers, or her mental health professional. These strategies are incorporated into the exercises in this book.

The exercises we've looked at so far will have encouraged your child to see how her self-defeating beliefs don't really help her. Ideally, this realization is helping to motivate her to begin to change some of those beliefs. The following exercise provides an opportunity to explicitly introduce your child to a program of transformation using CBT. By engaging her senses, she will come to see how CBT makes sense and how it can help her.

EXERCISE: Detectives, Wizards, and Winners—Oh, My!

Start by collecting the following items: a detective's hat (any hat that makes your child feel like a detective), a magic wand (available at party or joke stores, or easily made with tape and a pencil (or the cardboard tube from a metal clothes hanger), a stuffed heart (available in card stores or toy stores), and a toy trophy. These items will help externalize inner processes for your child and help her to understand the basics of the CBT approach used in this book. The detective hat will symbolize her ability to discover thoughts that create emotions and behaviors; the magic wand will symbolize her capacity to imagine a better outcome; the stuffed heart will symbolize her feelings; and the trophy will represent her changed behavior.

Invite your child to play a game called the "Sherlock Holmes game" or the "detective game." Describe to your child that, like sleuths, you're going to work together to find and uncover the beliefs that cause problems and change those beliefs to create the outcomes that she wants.

Briefly describe CBT theory in a way your child will understand. Explain that thoughts lead to emotions, which lead to behavior. Engage your child by setting up the game so it focuses on a concrete issue that she is struggling with. To make this fun for her, give her the detective's hat to wear as she tries to find the trail of thinking that has led to problematic feelings and behaviors.

Once your child has identified some specific thoughts that are creating problems, you can let her know that now she can pretend to be a wizard. (If your child loves the Harry Potter books, you can ask her to think about Harry Potter rather than just a generic wizard.) Give your child the magic wand, which represents her ability to imagine a better outcome. Ask her to pretend to be the wizard and tell you what magic she would create with the magic wand's unlimited powers. This is meant to help your child expand her thinking and imagine the most positive alternative outcome possible.

Once your child has imagined the best alternative outcome possible, you can show her how the heart symbolizes her feelings and how the trophy symbolizes her successful resolution of the problem. Invite her to think about how she would feel if she changed her problematic thoughts and how she could achieve the desired outcome.

For example, imagine that your child has come home complaining that she is doing terribly in her social studies class. Invite her to play the detective game, shaping it to match her interests and the situation. Give her the magic wand and ask her to make a wish regarding how she would like things to turn out. Then ask her what thoughts she would need to have in order to make that happen. You might invite her to put on the detective hat and investigate what she could say to herself that would help make her wish come true. She might identify thoughts like "I would have to believe that I could do better if I tried harder," or "I would have to believe that even though it's hard I can learn how to concentrate." Then you could ask her to hold the stuffed heart and identify how these thoughts would make her feel. She might realize that by believing that she can achieve her goals through hard work she'll feel more hopeful or determined to do better. Then you can use the trophy to symbolize a concrete behavior that would help make her wish come true. For example, you might help your child identify that if she worked on social studies for one hour each night, she would be more likely to achieve her wish.

As you can see, by engaging your child's senses and imagination, you will have much more luck in making these exercises interesting for your child and using one of her intense interests in the games.

The Challenge of Self-Blame

Because having a child with ADHD affects the whole family, you, your partner, your diagnosed child, and your other children will benefit if you apply some of the principles of CBT to yourself. Because of your engagement in the mental health and school systems, you may have come to feel as if you have made some serious mistakes as a parent or that you are somehow to blame for your child's difficulty. And this feeling can have a serious negative impact on you as you may begin to doubt not only your abilities as a parent but your own worth. You may begin to feel that you're not good enough or that no matter how hard you try, you cannot do well as a parent. You may begin to feel inferior to other parents. You may feel ashamed when meeting with teachers and doctors about your child's behavior.

If you start to feel depressed and lose interest in activities that you used to enjoy, you can benefit from trying some of these cognitive behavioral interventions on yourself. Because your child with ADHD is so sensitive, she will be dramatically affected by your state of mind. Recent research has shown that a mother's depression has a serious impact on her child's behavior. The good news is that when a mother's depression improves, the child's behavior improves too. According to pediatric psychiatrist Scott Shannon, "Researchers also found that kids of moms with improved depression showed marked reductions in their symptoms. A full third of the labeled kids lost their labels when their moms got better" (2007, 49). So anything you can do to help yourself will indirectly help your child, in part because as you help yourself you will be more patient and loving toward your child. You will also have more energy to spend quality time with your child and build the relationship that will be the foundation for coping with and transforming the diagnosis of ADHD.

To make things worse, some of the popular literature on ADHD blames parents for the child's disorder, pinning the genesis of the problem on parental abuse or neglect. Also, teachers wishing to shift the blame away from the way they manage their classroom may be too eager to place the blame on parents. But even if you've never read any of this literature or been blamed for the diagnosis by a teacher, you may have been haunted by the fear that somehow you are culpable. Mothers are particularly prone to feeling responsible and may even wonder if ADHD was the result of something they did while they were pregnant. For a parent, the potential sources of self-blame are endless. Be assured that these are normal reactions, but there is much you can do to counter these notions and feel better. And, as you help yourself, you will also be helping your child.

Try to remember that the more you blame yourself, the more you'll feel guilty about your child's ADHD, and the more your energy will be diverted away from helping your child. It can sometimes be difficult to see how this dynamic works, as guilt pulls at your attention. The next exercises will help you discover how guilt and self-blame work against your efforts to help your child thrive.

EXERCISE: The Costs and Benefits of Self-Blame

What do you gain by blaming yourself? Consider all the ways you may benefit from self-blame, and write them in a notebook. For example, perhaps by blaming yourself you feel like you are more in control of the situation. Perhaps you feel less helpless by taking responsibility for the ADHD diagnosis. Try to generate as many benefits as possible by asking yourself these prompting questions:

- What are the benefits to my child diagnosed with ADHD?

- What are the benefits to my spouse?

- What are the benefits to my other children?

- What are the benefits to my professional well-being?

- What are the benefits to my health?

Now consider the costs of self-blame, making a list in your notebook. For example, perhaps you feel worse about yourself as a parent as a result of blaming yourself. Perhaps you spend valuable time ruminating about how you have failed your child. Perhaps you are afraid of interacting with your child for fear that you might make another mistake. Try to generate as many possible negative effects of your self-blame as you can. Ask yourself these questions:

- What are the costs to my child diagnosed with ADHD?

- What are the costs to my spouse?

- What are the costs to my other children?

- What are the costs to my professional well-being?

- What are the costs to my health?

Examine your list of costs and benefits of taking blame for your child's diagnosis. Most likely you have arrived at the conclusion that it is to your benefit and your family's benefit to stop blaming yourself. Now, remember that your thoughts will ultimately change your feelings. Next time you find yourself feeling guilty, remind yourself that there are no substantial benefits and many costs of self-blame. Regardless of the truth or falsity of the charge, self-blame is simply not productive. Further, one concrete way you can assist your child's transformation is to stop blaming yourself. This will help you gain control in a situation where you often find yourself feeling helpless.

If you find that, no matter what you do, you cannot relieve yourself of feeling guilty, you can try the following exercise.

EXERCISE: Facing Your Worst Fears

Ask yourself the following questions. Write your responses in your notebook.

1. Am I to blame for my child's ADHD?

2. If it is true that I am to blame, then what is the worst thing that will happen? (For example, perhaps you fear that your child will be taken away from you.)

Now, look at your answer to question 1. Ask yourself what evidence you have that this conclusion is true. Write the evidence in your notebook. Next, ask yourself what evidence you have that it is false. Write the evidence for that in your notebook.

You'll most likely find that your fears are essentially irrational, with almost no evidence to support them. For example, if you asked yourself, "What if it is true that I am a terrible mother?" and you replied that you should have your children taken away from you, then you would likely see how ridiculous your deepest fears are, because there is almost certainly no evidence to support that statement.

Similarly, you will probably be able to generate a wealth of reasons why you are *not* a terrible mother. For example, you may be able to see that your child is healthy and happy despite her struggles with the diagnosis, that you love your child, and that you both enjoy the time you spend together.

As you shift your understanding of ADHD from that of a disorder to that of a gift, you will begin to shift from taking the blame to taking the credit for having nurtured such a gifted, unique child.

EXERCISE: Give Yourself Credit

Self-blame can become like a bad virus that spreads and infects the way you perceive everything else. You may develop a tendency to see all the ways in which you are a failure as a parent. If you blame yourself, you may not be aware of and recognize all of the times you're a great parent. In order to counteract this tendency it is important that you increase your awareness of your strengths as a parent. Try the following exercise:

1. Reflect on your parenting over the past week. Write down all of the specific things you did as a parent that were loving and caring.

2. Complete the following sentence: My child is lucky to have me as a parent because _____ .

3. As you move forward into this next week, keep a log of all the loving, caring, and helpful things you do, say, or think as a parent. You may want to buy a small notebook to keep with you so you don't forget any of your great parenting moments. Be sure to pay attention and look for ways in which you give to your children and care for yourself so you'll have more to give your children. Be as specific, concrete, and thorough as possible. Do not leave anything out. You might even find yourself thinking that you are grateful to be a parent. If you do, write that down—it counts.

SUMMARY

In this chapter we reviewed some general strategies for beginning to transform your child's problems into strengths. The main techniques of CBT involve challenging negative thoughts, examining the evidence for negative expectations, generating positive expectations for you and your child, and reframing negative traits and expectations as positive ones. This chapter reviewed some general strategies, including CBT techniques, that will guide you through many of the exercises in the rest of the book.

CHAPTER 3

Reclaiming Self-Esteem for Your Child

Self-esteem is your child's fundamental sense of being worthy, of deserving respect, and of respecting others. A child with a healthy self-esteem does not feel less than other people, nor does he feel better than anyone else. Central to transforming your child's problems into strengths is that your child develop a realistic and positive self-esteem. He needs to regain a sense that he is able to change outcomes in the world by changing his behavior. He needs to learn that he is powerful and not fundamentally flawed because of the diagnosis of ADHD—that he has much to offer his teachers, peers, siblings, and parents.

Because of both the insulting sound of the diagnosis of ADHD and his repeated experiences of failure in school, your child's self-esteem is doubly at risk. It's important for you as a parent to be aware of these threats, which jeopardize your child's ability to both feel good about himself and believe that he should keep working hard to achieve his goals. You have the power to identify your child's self-doubt and to change it. To help you, we will review threats to your child's self-esteem, not in order to scare you but so you can look out for the signs that he may be losing confidence in himself and then step in and help turn his thoughts around.

Your child may feel inferior to other students because he often gets negative feedback from teachers and other students. He may feel inferior because he notices he is having a harder time succeeding than the other students. It may seem as though schoolwork and behaviors such as sitting still come so much easier for others. It is easy for your child to make the leap to believing that he is less worthy than other students because of these difficulties. The loss of a sense of positive self-worth and the feeling of being inferior to others causes many behavioral disturbances and academic and social disturbances, which look a lot like ADHD. As you can imagine, this dynamic can create a vicious circle: the traits of ADHD lead to low self-esteem, which leads to increased severity of the traits, which then continues the cycle of lowering self-esteem.

In this chapter, after examining how self-esteem is the fundamental building block in transforming your child's problems into strengths, we'll review a wide range of exercises for enhancing your child's self-esteem.

SELF-EFFICACY

While your child's self-esteem reflects how he feels about his general worth, his *self-efficacy* reflects specific beliefs about his ability to make changes in his life. Self-efficacy is a component of self-esteem. Your child's sense of self-efficacy is the set of beliefs and attitudes he has about his power to make his dreams come true. If your child has strong self-efficacy it means that he believes that if he wants to do better in school, he can work harder and do better. It means that if he wants to get along more smoothly with other students, he knows he can try harder, learn social skills, and make friends. The opposite of self-efficacy is learned helplessness, in which a person learns that his efforts won't achieve the intended results. If your child believes that no matter how hard he tries he won't do better in school, he will simply stop trying. If he believes that no matter what he does he will never be popular with other students, he will act out aggressively toward others. The most important belief to instill in your child, after respecting himself and others, is that he can create and change his reality.

Children with ADHD are at risk for giving up, thereby making their symptoms worse and reducing their self-efficacy. Researchers have shown that children with ADHD are less persistent in academic tasks than children who do not have this diagnosis (Hoza et al. 2001), in part because they begin to believe that they do not have what it takes to succeed. This chapter will show how the diagnosis of ADHD creates or exacerbates some of its characteristic symptoms by lowering self-efficacy. Exercises later in this chapter will help your child believe he has the power to create the outcomes he wants.

Avoiding Rejection: Self-Protective Measures

As we've discussed, all of the traits of ADHD can be seen as differences rather than problems. But because these traits elicit responses of rejection from others, they get translated into problems that become more severe as the child's self-esteem falls. Your child's behavior has a certain logic to it: it can be seen as a predictable response of a sensitive child to an environment in which he has experienced repeated failures. Through accepted theories about how people learn and adapt, we know that people are motivated to avoid situations that are painful. So, if school has become painful and your child cannot physically leave the environment, he will adopt strategies for mentally leaving (inattention) or for changing the environment in disruptive ways to express his anger and feelings of rejection.

By understanding your child's behavior as a strategy for coping with feelings of low self-esteem and low self-efficacy, you are empowered to transform your child. You can help your child by trying the exercises in this chapter to change his fundamental beliefs about how powerful he is.

Before we get to the exercises, let's take a brief look at how the specific symptoms of ADHD can be caused or exacerbated by low self-esteem and low self-efficacy. The symptoms listed below match the criteria used to make a diagnosis of ADHD.

SELF-HANDICAPPING: RESPONSE TO NEGATIVE FEEDBACK

Negative feedback may cause your child to give up trying, or to *self-handicap*. Self-handicapping may be a strategy your child has developed to protect his self-esteem. This ineffective coping strategy can sometimes result from learned helplessness. If your child fails at something and can believe that he didn't really try, he can hold on to the possibility that he would do well if he did try. In the face of consistent and frequent negative feedback, children are likely to adopt self-defeating coping styles to protect some remnant of self-respect. Other symptoms of ADHD, such as losing things, not following through on instructions, and forgetfulness, can also be seen as aspects of your child's strategy to protect himself through self-handicapping.

DIFFICULTY MAINTAINING ATTENTION AND FOLLOWING THROUGH

As we'll discuss in later chapters, the label "attention deficit" usually means that children are not focusing on what teachers and adults want them to. Children are always paying attention to something, but it might be their own daydreams or the boy sitting next to them in class rather than the teacher's lessons. Although this kind of creative focusing can be seen as a strength, it can definitely be seen as a problem in the classroom, and problematic aspects of this trait develop from the child's feeling helpless to change his experience.

How does this happen? If your child has given up hope that he can succeed through sustained effort, then often he will direct his attention toward other things, in an effort to avoid the painful experience of receiving negative feedback. This is an effect of the "why try?" attitude that results from repeated failure.

FIDGETING

High energy and exuberance is certainly a strength, but it becomes problematic and disruptive for your child when he continually receives negative feedback. In turn, hyperactivity and fidgeting may become a way for your child to avoid being mindful of a painful or uncomfortable environment—being continually "on the go" is a way of distracting himself from the awareness that in that environment he is not appreciated for who he is.

Somewhere within himself, your child knows that his differences represent a potential strength and that the rejection he faces in the school system represents an injustice. As a child, he is not equipped to fully understand why he feels so rejected just for being himself. He protects himself from full awareness of these feelings, which would be terribly painful, by acting out and staying on the move.

DISRUPTIVE BEHAVIOR AND IMPATIENCE

Hyperactive behavior may be a way for your child to distract himself from the pain of his predicament, but disruptive behavior is the expression of his anger at the injustice of the situation—and it's also a self-protective strategy. If a child has repeatedly been told that his differences are a deficit and has come to believe that he is somehow inferior to his peers, he may be motivated to disrupt the environment out of a sense of anger. It's almost as if your child is saying, "If this environment rejects me, I'll show it!" Disrupting the classroom, teachers, and peers is a behavioral way of rejecting the environment first.

ENHANCING SELF-ESTEEM

As we have discussed, the main way to enhance your child's self-esteem is to reframe the diagnosis of ADHD as a strength. Chapters 5 through 9 will detail the five gifts of ADHD and will reframe the symptoms as positive traits.

This idea is not just a rosy view of an otherwise problematic condition. In recent years, the world has changed dramatically in ways that even give a child with ADHD an advantage. In *A Whole New Mind*, Daniel Pink (2005, 2–3) writes, "The capabilities we once disdained or thought frivolous—the "right-brain" qualities of inventiveness, empathy, joyfulness, and meaning—increasingly will determine who flourishes and who flounders." These capabilities closely match the gifts I outline in this book: creativity, ecological consciousness, interpersonal intuition, exuberance, and emotional sensitivity.

It is important, however, that your child's self-esteem be realistic. You don't want to create inflated positive expectations for your child that will lead him to continued disappointment. Sometimes children with ADHD act with bravado and overestimate their scholastic competence as a protective mechanism (Owens and Hoza 2003). If your child has an unrealistic positive sense of his academic performance, it may actually undermine his persistence on tasks. Actually, children may adopt this unrealistic belief in order to justify not persisting. ADHD children who have consistent patterns of low achievement may tell their parents, "I don't need to study for the quiz. I know all the material, and I'll do great!" If this is the pattern your child displays, you will want to work toward increasing his self-esteem while encouraging a realistic sense of how much work he needs to do. The point is to protect and nurture your child's ability to persist and his confidence in his capacity to accomplish success.

Success, it is said, is 99 percent hard work and 1 percent inspiration. Children with a diagnosis of ADHD have a harder time staying focused for long periods of time, have less motivation to try harder because they think they are handicapped, and are likely to underestimate how much persistent effort and hard work is necessary for success. The following exercises will help your child address these tendencies so they do not become deficits.

EXERCISE: Accepting That I Am Different

In this exercise you will help your child to realistically accept that he's different. You will also guide him to have a compassionate response to his difference rather than getting mad at himself for being different.

1. Ask your child what having ADHD means to him. Let him respond as much or as little as he wants. Answer any questions, but try to get a sense of how he feels about the diagnosis. Turn this into a game by showing your child how he can use one of his hands to share with you how his heart feels. Hold your hand out in a tight fist and say, "When someone tells me I did something wrong, my heart closes down and feels like this." Then, open your hand with the palm up, like a bowl, and say, "When someone says I'm great just the way I am, my heart feels like this."

2. Now ask your child to show you with his hand how his heart feels when the teacher says he is disrupting class or scolds him for not paying attention. If your child says he cannot do it or does not know what his heart is feeling, ask him to take a couple of breaths and concentrate on his heart area. If he still does not know what you want, tell him to just pretend. Remind him that there is no right or wrong answer—this is just a game of make-believe. After he shows you how his heart feels by using his hand, ask him to show you what his heart feels like when the teacher notices he is trying very hard and is pleased with him.

3. Now ask your child to show you with his hand how his heart feels when he hears that he has ADHD. He will probably have a closed fist. Ask him to tell you why his heart is closed. Ask

51

him what he needs in order to open his heart. Listen to him and make note of changes you can make in the home and in the school setting.

4. Tell your child that ADHD is something that makes a person different, but that differences are good and the difference of ADHD is a gift. Tell your child that because he is different from other children this sometimes makes life harder for him. Tell him that he can take one of two different attitudes about the diagnosis: (1) he can be mad at others for not having the diagnosis and he can feel sorry for himself for being different, or (2) he can realize how strong he is for making it through school when he is different from what the school leaders expect of children. He can realize that his traits make him really good at some things, and that his differences can serve the world in important, needed ways.

5. Ask your child to show you with his hand how each of these beliefs makes his heart feel. Likely he will show you that the first one makes his heart close up and the second one makes his heart open. Tell him that he will want to focus on repeating the second option to himself in order to keep his heart open.

Rewarding Effort

One way to work toward increasing self-esteem is to encourage your child to praise himself for making a real effort. If the child learns to reward himself for his efforts, his persistence will increase. On the other hand, if he were to praise himself only for successful outcomes, he might not have as much chance to reinforce himself in the beginning and would likely get frustrated; he might even begin to value himself for his outcomes rather than his effort, which would in turn lead to negative thoughts about himself. So, because your child's diagnosis is a difference that is at odds with most current school settings, he needs to learn to reward himself based on his efforts.

It's also important that you learn to reward your child for his efforts at improving his schoolwork, relationships with others, and behavior. You can do this by committing to noticing when he's trying and letting him know that you see his efforts. Give him verbal praise. On occasion, you can reward him with whatever goodies are motivating to him, whether it be a special snack, a dinner out at his favorite restaurant, or a trip to the park. Here's an exercise that reinforces the idea of making an effort.

EXERCISE: Try-Hard Bingo

This strategy is an example of what's called *behavioral management.* Of all psychological theories about how to change people, behavioral management is acknowledged as the most effective way of transforming behaviors. Researchers have found that rewarding people for good behaviors increases those behaviors, and punishing people for bad behaviors decreases those. This powerful strategy for change is effective with animals, little kids, the elderly, and almost any other population or culture you can imagine. However, in this book, we will focus on rewarding increased efforts. This book does not include any exercises that use punishment of bad behavior. Because they are rewarded, the positive behaviors tend to become so prevalent that the bad behaviors eventually get edged out.

In this exercise, you make a game out of rewarding your child for making positive efforts.

In your notebook, make a bingo card like the one on the next page. Tell your child that you will be playing a game of Try-Hard Bingo, in which he can get credit just for trying harder. Explain the rules of bingo, but tell him that in this game he will get a star if he can report one incidence of trying hard in one of the domains. Each day he will have a chance to earn stars. He wins if he gets a star in every domain on any one day or in one domain every day of the week. Each week, work out what the bingo prize will be for a day or a domain. For example, on any day that he shows that he tried hard in every domain, he gets to watch an extra half hour of TV, and for any domain that he shows that he tried hard every day of the week, he gets five dollars.

Try-Hard Bingo Card		
	Schoolwork	Relationships	Behavior
Monday			
Tuesday			
Wednesday			
Thursday			
Friday			
Saturday			
Sunday			

To make this game more successful, give your child a chance to think about what rewards would be motivating. Let him make a long list, and talk with him about all the things he would like that would be pleasurable. Of course, you'll have to set limits. You wouldn't want your child to be allowed to eat pizza every night. But, within limits, agree on a wide range of rewards that are reasonable from your perspective and motivating for him. By giving your child a lot of time to think about and talk about all the things he likes to have and to do, you'll make the game more fun. You might even come up with a reward scheme in which the Try-Hard Bingo card for each week lists a different reward for each day and for each domain. In this way, your child's interest will be maintained, and he will be motivated each day of the week and in each domain.

Keep a copy of the Try-Hard Bingo card displayed prominently at home. Also give your child a copy to take to school with him. Ask him to try to be aware of every time that he tries harder to persist in schoolwork, to gain skills for getting along with other children, or to manage his behavior when he doesn't feel like it. Ask him to write down in a notebook how he tried and what he did, in each of the domains—schoolwork, relationships, or good behavior.

Every night, spend some time reviewing your child's notebook and filling out the Try-Hard Bingo card. On any night that you check off all three domains (you might want to use stickers or stars), make a big deal of giving your child the prize for that day. At the end of the week, determine whether your child has won bingo in the domain of schoolwork, relationships, or behavior. If so, offer lots of praise and the prize for that domain.

Change Your State—Make It Great!

Often, low self-esteem occurs in children with the diagnosis of ADHD when they feel that they are out of control in their lives. They often have good intentions, and they feel upset as they are called to account for their bad behavior. Low self-esteem may result also from being in a low mood, from feeling blue about being out of control, or from the cascade of negative feedback they get in school and from peers.

One of the quickest ways to give your child self-esteem is to show him that he is in charge of his own state of mind. You can show him that, no matter what happens, he can control his internal reactions and feelings. And the quickest way for any person—adult or child—to change his state of mind is to pay attention to his breathing. The second-quickest way is to change body posture. The following exercises can be played as a game with your child, to show him how he can change his mood in minutes.

EXERCISE: The Be-a-Balloon Game

Before starting the game, ask your child to rate how he feels on a scale of 1 to 10. Tell him that 1 means feeling pretty lousy and 10 means feeling awesome.

Remind your child of the balloons he has seen in parades, such as Underdog in the Macy's Thanksgiving Day Parade, or any other inflatable toy he may have seen. Tell him to sit in a chair and pretend that he is Underdog on the day before the parade—he is just an empty, limp balloon. You can demonstrate by sitting in a chair with your arms, shoulders, and head hanging down. Tell him that you feel like a rag doll, loose and heavy.

Ask him to take a deep breath and imagine that he is being filled with air and is expanding. Play along with him and demonstrate. As you are being filled with air, stick out your chest, raise your hands in the air as if they are being filled with air, and raise your head. Imagine an inflatable person being filled with air, and tell your child to imagine this also. When your child is "fully inflated," say, "Hold it for one, two, three—and release, blowing out all your breath." As you expel the air, make a "whewww" sound, as if air is being let out of a balloon. Tell your child that when he releases the air, he is to collapse again in a relaxed, loose, and heavy position.

Practice this exercise two more times. After you have done it three times, ask your child how he feels now on a scale of 1 to 10, with 1 being pretty lousy and 10 being awesome. It is likely that the number will be higher than the one he started with. Point out to your child that his number went up and that he was able to make that happen just by breathing and changing his posture.

Show your child how he can do this in a smaller way, without pretending to be a parade balloon—demonstrate how to take a deep breath, hold it for a count of three, and release. He can do this anytime he feels anxious, feels upset, or has hurt feelings. This exercise will show him that he's in control of his state of mind. Also, show him that he can raise his head and hold his shoulders back, and that just this change will improve his mood and cause others to respond to him in a more positive way.

EXERCISE: Act Like Your Favorite Superstar

This exercise will tap into your child's imagination, which can seem to be on overdrive all the time, and channel it to help him change to a positive state of mind. As in the preceding exercise, the important point is for him to learn that he can—through simple and quick games—change his emotional state very quickly. Through these skills, he will learn that he is in charge, and that other people cannot control him.

Sometimes parents get worried when their child seems to have an obsession with a sports star, a movie star, or a fictional character. However, usually this type of preoccupation is an attempt at self-healing for your child. And you can use his interest in this person or character to your child's advantage—the superstar your child has latched onto can be used as an inspiration and motivational force. You can use your child's preoccupation with this person to engage his interest in exercises to help transform his problems into strengths. While your child will not likely be motivated to engage in a behavioral management program per se, any game that involves his hero will provide a lot of energy and motivation for the exercise, and it will provide one more arena where you can work with your child's interests rather than against him.

Of course, you will have to use your judgment. Typically, children's heroes are characters like Harry Potter, sports figures like Lance Armstrong, or mythical figures like knights in shining armor. If for some reason your child's hero is a villain-type figure, you may want to move on to another exercise. Throughout this book you will be given more than enough exercises for each problem you're trying to address; do not push an exercise if you or your child doesn't like it or it doesn't fit for some reason. If your child responds to only a handful of the exercises presented in this book, you will still see dramatic changes that will stop his spinning out of control.

It is best to demonstrate this exercise when your child is upset, angry, or hurt, so you can demonstrate his power to change his state. Say, "Let me show you who is in control of how you feel. Tell me on a scale of 1 to 10, with 1 being terrible and 10 being awesome, how you feel right now."

Next, tell him to think of his favorite superstar and to hold a posture like that of the character or person. If it's a book or movie character, ask him to choose a pose from a moment or scene that is particularly heroic. Tell your child to stand like the superstar, pretend like he is that superstar, and feel all the feelings of that superstar. Tell him that for the next two minutes he should walk, talk, and act like the superstar.

After two minutes, ask your child how he feels different. Ask him how he feels on a scale of 1 to 10. It is likely that he will have changed his feelings, thoughts, and attitudes just by pretending to be his favorite superstar.

Helping Your Child Reclaim Control

Children with an ADHD diagnosis have a more difficult time controlling their behavior than other children do. It often seems that words fly out and behaviors erupt without any filtering, and these inappropriate behaviors are often disruptive to others. To make matters worse, sometimes the diagnosis of ADHD, because it sounds like a medical disorder, increases your child's belief that he cannot control his own behavior. It is almost as if the ADHD diagnosis gives your child permission to act out and justification for bad behavior once it's occurred. Feeling like you can control your behavior, your thoughts, and your attitudes is a central component of self-esteem. In addition to learning to manage his behavior, your child needs to believe that he is capable of controlling his actions. The following pretend game will help your child reclaim his belief in his own power.

EXERCISE: The Coach and the Cheerleader

Set up this exercise by telling your child that, like any sports superstar, he needs to have a coach and a cheerleader to do his best. Tell him that you want to play a pretend game with him where he learns to be his own coach and cheerleader. Any toys or props you can add to the game will make it more fun. You could make some pom-poms and a bullhorn out of paper for the cheerleader. For the coach you could get a baseball cap or a toy whistle. If there is a specific team, sport, or player that your child admires, see if you can find a team jersey for him to wear and make this exercise come alive.

Start by asking your child to tell you how a coach and a cheerleader help sports players. Generate as many answers as possible. You will want to make sure to include the following points:

- A coach tells players how to handle certain problems during a game.

- A coach makes the players practice, practice, practice.

- A coach tells the players what to expect.

- A coach gives the players strategies to prepare for game day.

- A coach gives pep talks to the players.

- A coach will challenge a player if the player has wrong ideas.

- A cheerleader gives a lot of support to the players.

- A cheerleader says nice things to the players.

- A cheerleader keeps hope up when the team is not winning the game.

- A cheerleader never gives up on the team.

Pick a concrete problem that occurred recently in your child's life and show him how to be a cheerleader or coach for himself. For example, if your son got in trouble for hitting his pencil against his desk and disrupting class this week, that would be a good situation to start with. Following is an example of how to do this. We'll call the child "Marty" for the sake of this exercise.

Mom: What did you say to yourself when the teacher asked you to stop hitting the desk with your pencil?

Marty: I told the teacher I was trying, but I said to myself that I couldn't stop. I didn't know what else to do with myself.

Mom: Okay, I'm going to pretend that I'm a cheerleader. (Mom takes out a paper bullhorn.) "Go, Marty. You can do it. Yes, you can! You can stop hitting your pencil on the desk if you want to. You have the power, Marty. If you try hard, you can do anything you want!" Now I'm going to be the coach. (Puts on a coach's baseball hat and blows a toy whistle.) "Hey, Marty, in order to win this game, take a deep breath and calm down. Try taking a couple of deep breaths and relax. That will help you win the game. Act like you're a rag doll, and go limp. Let your body relax; feel heavy and warm. Remember to breathe!" Okay, how do you feel now?

Marty: I feel better. I feel like, if I tried, I could do better in class.

The next step is to reverse roles. You act out the same problematic behavior (in this case, hitting a pencil against the desk), and your child pretends to be the coach and the cheerleader. The following is an example of how to do this.

Mom: Okay, I'm Marty, and I'm in class. (Mom has fun pretending to be Marty. She sits down with a pencil and begins hitting it against a table.) Why's everyone looking at me and why's that teacher telling me to quiet down and stop hitting my pencil on the desk? I like the noise—it helps me calm down. It's so boring in here! I can't stop anyway—I have ADHD.

Marty: Hey, Marty, you can do it. You can stop hitting the pencil on the desk if you want. Why don't you calm down by taking a deep breath? You can do the balloon exercise and fill yourself up with air. That would be another way to calm down. Go, Marty! You can do it!

Mom: But that teacher is so mean to me. If I stop, she wins. She embarrassed me in front of the whole class.

Marty: Hey, Marty, you win if you stop hitting the pencil on the desk, because then you show that you can control yourself. Don't let the teacher bring you down. Focus on you. You can do it. You can control yourself.

Mom: Great job being coach and cheerleader, Marty!

Tell your child that he can be the cheerleader and the coach for himself any day and time he needs support and encouragement. Tell him that everybody needs both a coach and a cheerleader with them at all times, but that he has to provide that support for himself.

Get out some 3 by 5 index cards and together create coach and cheerleader cards. Apply your creativity and have fun using stickers, markers, and crayons so that the cards are fun to look at. On one side, each card should say "Coach" or "Cheerleader." On the other side you should write a statement that will help your child believe he can control his behavior or use a specific strategy.

Some examples of statements on coach cards are below:

- Show respect and appreciation for your teacher's hard work.

- You win if you keep trying!

- Take a deep breath and calm down!

- The harder you try, the smarter you get!

- You can build your brain by working harder!

- Look at your teacher and listen!

- Pretend you're a rag doll. Feel your body as it gets warm and heavy. This will help you sit still.

Some examples of statements on cheerleader cards are the following:

- You can do it!

- You have the power! Try harder!

- Keep going! Keep trying!

- You can control your behavior!

- You are in charge!

- You win if you control your actions!

Your child can take these cards to school with him to teach him how to talk to himself. The cards will be more effective if they are specific to particular problems. For example, if the teacher repeatedly complains that your son cannot sit still, you can create cheerleader cards that say, "I can sit still."

SUMMARY

This chapter offered many different strategies for helping your child improve his self-esteem and his ability to try harder in managing his behavior. Remember that if you or your child does not like the exercises, it's best not to push them. They will only work if you and your child have fun with them. You don't need to do every exercise to transform your child. If only a couple of these games work well for both you and your child, then do those two exercises repeatedly. Also, keep in mind that the more creative and fun you can be in creating these games, the more success you will have. Your child has an immense capacity for imagination, and the more you rely on that imagination in pretend games—rather than moralizing about the right way to behave—the more you will engage your child's attention. The fun you have together will also help you build a strong relationship with him that will become the foundation for transforming his problems into strengths.

CHAPTER 4

How to Become Your Child's Advocate, Not Apologist

The key ingredient in transforming your child's diagnosis into a gift is your relationship with her. What your child needs more than anything is for you to be on her side. After that, what your child needs is for you to bring her teachers and mental health professionals over to her side too. In short, your child needs you to become her advocate. Your support for your child will improve her behavior. Kids tend to misbehave when they feel mad, sad, or alone. As you support your child, these negative feelings, which drive bad behavior, will go away.

BARRIERS TO BECOMING YOUR CHILD'S ADVOCATE

Advocating for your child may have been difficult for you to do until now. This chapter offers exercises that will make this task easier, and specific strategies for improving your effectiveness at advocacy. It is important that you not blame yourself for how you have interacted with your child in the past. It's also important that you not beat yourself up for the times that you've failed to move forward. Many things may have stood in the way of your becoming a forceful advocate, and many parents feel all too ready to take on guilt about their kid's struggles. To help relieve you of some of this self-blame and remind you of the real challenges you've been facing, we will review the significant barriers that may have made it difficult for you to act as your child's advocate.

More Than a Handful

The first barrier that's made it difficult for you to become your child's advocate is that, most likely, your child really is a handful. In fact, your child may be more than a handful. All young children are energetic and rambunctious compared to their parents and teachers. But it's quite possible that your child has even more energy than a typical child. In some ways, your child is like a 50-watt lightbulb that has 100 watts of energy coursing through it.

Your child has a hard time managing her high levels of energy. You, the parent, have to manage not only your child's high levels of energy but also her difficulties managing her energy, despite the fact that you do not have an enormous amount of energy yourself. In short, children with ADHD can be exhausting for adults. Out of sheer fatigue, you may have found yourself being short tempered with your child. Or you may have found yourself using strategies that you know will not be helpful to her in the long run.

Because you may have your own complaints about the difficulties managing such a live wire, you may have become an apologist for your child in interacting with others, including teachers. For example, when the teacher has complained about your child's behavior, you may have found it easy to apologize to the teacher. You may feel guilty, thinking that your child's teacher considers you a bad parent, so you have to show him that it's not your fault by apologizing for your child. Your own exhaustion and frustration are probably among the barriers you have faced that can prevent you from becoming an advocate for your child. Later in this chapter we will review why, although you may be sympathetic with complaints about your child, you will need to gently challenge those complaints. See the section below, "What to Do When the Teacher Calls," for a cheat sheet of ways to handle calls or complaints from the teacher. If your child has already been diagnosed with ADHD, this section will help you advocate for your child. If your child has not been diagnosed with ADHD, but the teacher is seeking a diagnosis, this section will help you feel confident that all other sources of disruptive behavior have been ruled out.

What to Do When the Teacher Calls: Stay Tuned to Your Child's Gifts

As parents, we love our kids so much, how can we not feel sick to our stomach when that fateful call comes—that call from the teacher saying that she thinks your child may have ADHD or that your child's behavior is causing problems in the classroom? Below are ten tips to remember if you get that call.

1. Realize that the call from the teacher is not a diagnosis. Teachers are not qualified to make a diagnosis. A diagnosis of ADHD requires a sophisticated data collection procedure from both parents and teachers and a trained mental health professional. Many other diagnoses need to be ruled out. If this procedure has not been followed, then it's not appropriate for the teacher to make this claim. There

are many reasons a child might have difficulty concentrating or be disruptive in class—the label of ADHD should be the last possible explanation explored, not the first.

2. Point to contexts that might be explanations for the behavior.

Many parents come to me near the end of the school year wondering what's wrong with their children. Sometimes kids know the end of the school year is coming and their mind begins to transition to summertime, and they lose focus. So, whatever time of year you get the call, remember to think about any possible external situation or context that might explain your child's behavior.

This is one component of "optimistic thinking." An optimist points to the external stressors to explain bad behavior rather than internalizing it. Is your child going through health challenges that might explain her behavior? Are any major changes happening at home? Stressors are usually the first and most probable explanation for disruptive behavior. For example, I know of children who were diagnosed with ADHD shortly after their parents divorced, but I always tell parents that it is difficult to make a reliable diagnosis of ADHD in the year following a divorce. The dramatic life changes are enough to explain disruptive behavior and changes in focus and attention.

So, if you get a call from a teacher who is concerned about your child, sit down and make a list of stressors happening in your family. These should include financial, family, health, and any reversals the child or family may have experienced. You want the teacher and yourself to see the roots of the problem rather than pointing to your child's brain and looking for a deficit disorder there.

3. Ask the teacher, "What are we going to do to support my child?"

In many areas of life, when we see a person having a

problem, we look for ways to support the person and identify basic skills that can be improved. If you put a child without practice out on a basketball court, you wouldn't diagnose her with Basketball Playing Deficit Disorder—you would recognize that she needed practice and some basic skills in order to effectively play basketball. What does this mean for your child? Children need to learn how to learn. Not every stumbling block in education is brain dysfunction. Your child may simply need much repetition, practice of basic skills, and coaching to excel in school.

4. Consider whether the school might be a poor match for your child.

If a creative artist went to work as an accountant for a Fortune 500 company, we would all know that she was headed for trouble. Sometimes our children's learning style and profile of strengths and weaknesses mean that they need accommodations. Many children who are natural athletes or artists struggle with the demands of school for reasons that have nothing to do with a brain disorder. In fact, some people argue that the whole education system is broken; they would say that we are preparing our kids for the global digital age in schools that were designed to prepare them for life during the Industrial Revolution.

If your school options are limited, you might refocus your goals on getting your child through school unscathed rather than hoping she will become a model student. You can protect the child's passion and motivation by supporting her in areas in which she is gifted or in which she has passionate interest and engagement.

5. Consider that slight adjustments might make big differences.

Sometimes making a small change can lead to big differences. One time I had a client who said, "I hate school."

When we explored deeply why he hated school, he said the teacher was always "dissing" him. When we continued to probe how the teacher "dissed" him, we realized that it came down to one daily event—the teacher positioned the child (my client) next to herself when the class walked as a group in the school building. My client thought that the teacher didn't trust him, but it turned out that he was the youngest child in the class and she always kept the "little ducklings" closest to her. When he realized that the teacher wasn't just "dissing" him, his attitude toward her and going to school changed. Just by listening to your child closely you can come up with some small changes, or offer new understanding, that will lead to big improvements.

6. Consider that other students or the teacher might not be a good match for your child.

    It is possible that the match between your child and the teacher or other children is creating problems. As adults, most of us have experienced being miserable because of a bad boss or unpleasant coworkers. But we adults have supports and power to make choices to turn around these difficult situations. The problem is that when a child has a personality conflict with a teacher or other students, we are quick to assume that it is entirely the child's fault, or that maybe there is something wrong with her brain. Our first approach should be to listen to the child's complaints about a teacher or student. Bullying does happen, and it has long-term negative consequences. Ask your child how she sees the problem—listen, and take it seriously.

7. Reflect: is this normal behavior in a child her age?

    Before you go looking for a brain disorder, you might want to consider whether the school or teacher has unreasonable expectations of students at your child's stage of development. For active boys, it is completely normal to display some rambunctious behavior. Teachers should be willing to acknowledge the need for activity and movement that all children have. There are many creative ways to channel physical energy, and doing so often can eliminate many so-called problems. Whatever happens, make sure that your child is not punished for a failure to sit still by having her recess or playtime taken away. Physical activity is not a symptom—it is a basic need for any child.

8. Look for explanations that do not involve your child's brain.

Even if you try all the techniques above and come to the conclusion that your child's behavior really is disturbed, you still don't have to land on the diagnosis of ADHD. There are many other explanations for symptoms and bad behavior that do not involve a brain disorder. Some things to consider are nutrition, your own mental health, and family stressors.

Many people ask me if I think poor nutrition causes ADHD. Though research does not support that poor nutrition causes ADHD, it is possible that it causes the misdiagnosis of ADHD. Look to the obvious—too much sugar, not eating breakfast, or other nutritional deficits can cause difficulty concentrating and poor behavior.

The family's mental health can play a role in a child's behavioral problems as well. If you or the child's other parent is depressed or struggling with addiction or any other mental health problem, that may be a likely explanation for your child's behavior. Your child receives emotional nourishment from her parents, so if you are having trouble, she may be taking in your emotional pain. Take a close look at how you are really doing; be honest with yourself and get help if you need it.

Sometimes the explanation for poor behavior in school is simple—the child needs more support. I have seen families solve the problems that led to a diagnosis of ADHD by getting tutoring or some other form of educational support. So if the teacher suggests that your child has ADHD, you can point to other things you will try before you open the door to the possibility of ADHD.

9. Focus on the positives.

When a teacher calls with any complaint about your child, it is important that you keep the positives about your child front and center in your own mind and in the teacher's mind. For example, many ADHD children are creative. They tend to generate ideas for interesting applications of the material they learn rather than feel motivated to memorize it and repeat it back on a quiz or worksheet. This cognitive process of creativity, *divergent thinking*, is a different type of learning style and one that is in great demand for solving the world's problems. Remember that your child's divergent thinking may someday be responsible for solving real-world problems and has great value.

In addition to creativity, the gifts of ADHD include but are not limited to emotional sensitivity, exuberance, interpersonal intuition, and connection to nature. Before you pick up the phone to return the teacher's call or go in for a personal meeting, create a list of your child's many gifts. Include a list of her intense interests, including artistic or athletic pursuits. This will help keep you and her teacher focused on her resources rather than the problem areas.

Think of it this way: every strength is a resource for patching up a weakness. Many children, if asked to come up with creative solutions to specific problems, are able to. For example, a child who needs to be physically active might bring a sponge to school and tap his pencil on the sponge so as not to disrupt other students while still feeding his need for activity.

10. Advocate for your child.

Research shows that your child's teacher will dramatically affect your child's actual outcomes in the classroom. This means you want to become an advocate for your child. Advocating means pointing out what your child is doing right and asking for support and resources for solving specific problems. You will want to get the teacher to be as specific as possible in his or her complaints and adopt a problem-solving approach, rather than suggesting that the child be evaluated for ADHD at the first sign of trouble. For example, if a teacher complains that your child is hyperactive and should get evaluated, ask for specific examples of this behavior and work toward solving the disruptions. A wiggly child can be given permission to leave his seat to go get a drink of water or get some materials from the principal's office, for instance.

The main action you can take to advocate for your child is to translate her "symptoms" into needs. For example, hyperactivity is a need for physical activity, and creativity is a need to explore novel applications and work toward novel solutions. In each case that your child's teacher points to a problem, you can try to find a way to translate it into a specific need that can be met with support from you and the school.

So remember, when the teacher calls, stay centered in your ability to protect your child by focusing on what's working and by using your child's gifts as the starting point for any conversation.

Iron-Clad Authority

Another barrier you may face is your own perception (or misperception) that teachers and mental health professionals are iron-clad authorities. If the teacher is saying that your child is a problem, you may think, "She must be right. After all, she sees lots of children and has a lot of points of comparison." If a mental health professional tells you that your child is disturbed, you may think, "He knows what he's talking about. He has studied this and is an expert on child behavior." But in both of these cases, you, not the educator or the doctor, are the expert on your child.

One of the reasons these authorities can be wrong about your child is that they are almost certainly working from a different paradigm. It doesn't matter how much knowledge or experience a person has—if he or she is working from an inaccurate perspective, then that person will not be the best judge of your child's behavior. For example, for many years the world's greatest astronomers looked at the skies with the understanding that the earth was the center of the universe. Although they were the experts, their fundamental worldview was wrong, and therefore they made many mistakes in their judgments. Similarly, this book offers a paradigm shift—or change in worldview—suggesting that ADHD is not a disorder but rather a gift.

If you can overcome the barrier of seeing teachers and other professionals as the final authority, then you can begin to advocate for your child by showing people how to see your child as you do. It may help you to remember that these experts may be right about the details but wrong about the big picture. For example, your child may jump out of her seat a lot during the school day and may interrupt other students. But these behaviors don't have to be seen as indicating that your child is fundamentally flawed. As you shift your own vision of your child, you can learn to help others who are involved in your child's life shift their view and so better serve your child.

Conflict Avoidance

You may have hesitated to advocate for your child because you were afraid of being thought of as adversarial or oppositional—the very same words that may sometimes be used to describe your child. Many people find it very difficult to confront others with a viewpoint that challenges what the other person is saying. Almost everyone is uncomfortable with disagreement. And many of us have a tendency to exaggerate our fears in our mind. For example, if your child's teacher says that your daughter is lazy, the apologist in you will want to apologize profusely to the teacher and promise to implement stricter controls in order to keep your child on top of her homework. In contrast, the advocate in you might say that you do not experience your child as lazy. Rather, you see her as very creative and have noticed that she is capable of intense effort when working on projects that involve her creativity.

As you imagine becoming an advocate for your child, you may become fearful that the teacher will get angry at you for contradicting him or her. You may worry that the teacher will think you are just being difficult and will assume that you are the cause of your child's problem. You may even worry that the teacher will be mad and take it out on your child. Or you may wonder if the teacher will think you are simply out of touch with reality. With practice, you will find that many of your fears are unfounded. Try the following exercise for coping with these concerns.

> **EXERCISE:** Challenging Your Fears
> of Being Challenging

1. In your journal or notebook, write down your major concerns about reframing your child's behavior to a complaining teacher. For example, you may be afraid that your child's teacher will think you are a bad parent.

2. Using a scale of 1 (very unlikely) to 10 (very likely), rate the likelihood that the thing you fear will actually happen.

3. Now write down thoughts that contradict your fear. Include all the positive things that may result from becoming an advocate for your child. For example, if you are afraid that your child's teacher will think you're a bad parent, you could write down that he might actually think you are a good parent for having such a positive view of your child. Or maybe the teacher would begin to see that your child has many positive traits that he hadn't noticed before. He might even start to give your child more positive attention in class.

4. Write down strategies you could use in order to cope if the thing you fear did come true; for example, if your child's teacher said to you, "No wonder your child is so difficult. It's obvious you are overprotective of her and oppositional to boot." In writing down coping strategies, you might write down specific responses to such a statement, such as "I know you don't have all the resources you need, but I want to make sure we've looked at all the angles here. Let's stay focused on what we can do to help my child."

5. After reviewing your coping strategies, set up a time to meet with your child's teacher who has given you negative feedback. Share with this teacher your different vision of your child. Emphasize your goal to become an advocate for your child so that she will have the best classroom experience possible. Affirm to the teacher that he has the same goals for serving your child, but that you may have different views about the nature of your child's behaviors.

6. After returning from your visit with the child's teacher, evaluate your original fears. Write down all of the positive outcomes of the meeting. For example, you might write that the teacher seemed really interested in your perspective on your child and that he did not get offended when you challenged his perspective. You

might also write that you hope that he will begin to see your child as gifted, give her more positive attention, and help her to improve in that class.

THE IMPORTANCE OF BECOMING AN ADVOCATE

Having reviewed why you might have had a difficult time in the past acting as an advocate for your child, you can let yourself off the hook. Be gentle with yourself as you move into this new role. In this section, we turn to the reasons it is so important that you become your child's advocate. By becoming her advocate you strengthen the foundational elements for transforming your child's problems into strengths—your relationship with your child, your child's environment, and your child's self-esteem.

Starting a Synergistic Cycle

As an advocate for your child, you will be starting a synergistic cycle that transforms symptoms into talents—or, at least, into lovable eccentricities. In a *synergistic* cycle, small changes work together to create larger changes. A small change in direction can begin a cycle that leads to more and more positive changes. This can work against the vicious circle that easily develops when negative views are taken of your child's symptoms. The synergistic cycle is made up of the following factors:

- As you advocate for your child, you feel empowered and maintain your positive view of her.

- As you feel better about yourself and your child, your interactions with her are more loving and rewarding for both of you.

- As your child feels loved and rewarded, she tries to show love through increased efforts at home and at school.

- As your child tries harder at school, she begins to experience more positive feedback.

- As she interacts with you in more loving ways, you find it easier to maintain your positive view and loving interactions.

- Finally, you and your child have a loving, close, connected relationship in which you work together and are on each other's side.

There will be a strong link between how supported your child feels by you and how hard she will try to work toward the goals that you and she have collaboratively set. The more you and your child work together, the more she will transform before your eyes and the easier it will be to create the connection you want. Also, by becoming an advocate for your child and offering teachers some alternatives and ideas, you will refocus your own energy in the direction that is most helpful for your child—toward your parent–child bond.

The opposite of the synergistic cycle is the vicious circle. The vicious circle that results when you act as an apologist for your child looks like this:

- You apologize for your child's behavior after a teacher gives you negative feedback.

- By accepting this negative feedback, you begin to see your child as essentially flawed.

- Seeing your child as flawed, you feel that you must have done something wrong, and you feel worse about yourself as a parent.

- Feeling inadequate as a parent, you are more likely to become angry or frustrated with your child.

- As your child gets negative feedback from you and feels a lack of closeness, she behaves in problematic ways to express her own distress.

- The more your child acts in problematic ways, the more negative feedback she gets at school, and the more frustrated you feel.

- The more frustrated you feel, the more difficult it is to feel connected to your child.

- You and your child both feel a growing distance between the two of you, and you begin to feel helpless and hopeless.

Becoming an advocate for your child means not accepting other people's negative evaluations of her. In addition, it gives you the opportunity to tactfully offer an alternative way of understanding your child to the teacher or health care professional. Below is an example of a dialogue in which the parent acts as an advocate and begins a synergistic cycle.

Teacher: Ms. Jones, thank you for taking the time to meet with me. As we discussed on the phone, Andrea has been a problem in class. She just doesn't seem to pay attention, and she talks to her friends during classroom exercises. This behavior is typical of ADHD students, and you should know that your daughter's behavior is out of control. Every time she does this, I have to stop class and tell her to sit in her seat and refrain from disturbing the whole class. After I warn her, her behavior seems to get worse.

Ms. Jones: Mr. Welch, thank you for your involvement with my daughter. I appreciate your concern for her well-being and development. I, too, want the best for her and want her to benefit from all that you have to offer students. I'm very close with my daughter, and I've noticed that recently she has overcome being rejected by her peers and is starting to bond with other girls, so her friendships are very meaningful to her. I think what you're describing might be the result of her insecurity about losing friendships. I wonder if, when you stop class and single her out, she feels embarrassed. Maybe you could try pulling her aside before class and gently let her know that her friends might feel distracted by her in-class conversations. In my experience, Andrea responds very well to coaching and gets embarrassed very easily. I wonder if you could try this approach and see if it works. It might be that singling her out in class is making her behavior worse. It seems worth a try.

Teacher: Hmm, I've never thought of it that way. I can try what you're suggesting and see how it works. I'll take her aside privately from now on. Thanks for your suggestion.

When Ms. Jones gets home, she feels empowered that she challenged the teacher respectfully. Ms. Jones tells Andrea she had the chance to talk to her teacher, Mr. Welch. She says that she told him that Andrea doesn't like to be embarrassed in front of the whole class and that Mr. Welch agreed not to do that anymore. Andrea feels important because her mom stood up for her to her teacher, and she resolves to make Mom proud of her by trying hard in Mr. Welch's class.

As you can see from this dialogue, by becoming an advocate for your child, you work to develop a positive interpretation of behaviors. In so doing you can change other people's perceptions of your child, and your own emotional reactions to her will be more positive. As you practice this, you will also feel more empowered. You won't spend your time worrying whether others think you are a bad parent—you will address the issue head-on and challenge it.

In contrast, the vicious circle of being an apologist for your child can look like the following.

Teacher: Ms. Jones, thank you for taking the time to meet with me. As we discussed on the phone, Andrea has been a problem in class. She just doesn't seem to pay attention, and she talks to her friends during classroom exercises. This behavior is typical of ADHD students, and you should know your daughter's behavior is out of control. Every time she does this, I have had to stop class and tell her to sit in her seat and refrain from disturbing the whole class. After I warn her, her behavior seems to get worse.

Ms. Jones: Mr. Welch, I'm so sorry that Andrea is acting out in class again. We're doing everything we can to help her. After I got your call, I called the psychiatrist. Maybe we can increase her medication. We're doing everything we can at home, but we're just at our wits' end.

Teacher: Well, I'm glad that you've made an appointment to check with the psychiatrist. Her behavior is disrupting the whole class and making my job nearly impossible.

Ms. Jones: (*Embarrassed, feeling like a bad parent.*) I'm so sorry. We will do everything we can at home to get her not to act out in class. I will be sure to tell her that she is disrupting your class and let her know that there will be serious consequences if she doesn't start behaving in school. In fact, I will tell her that if I get one more phone call from Mr. Welch, she'll have to miss a softball game.

Teacher: Well, thank you, Ms. Jones. I need as much support as I can get from parents at home in order to manage ADHD students. I'm glad we're on the same page.

Ms. Jones goes home feeling helpless and like a bad mom. She feels out of control and frustrated that, no matter what she does, Andrea doesn't seem to change. She goes home and gives Andrea a stern warning about what will happen if she continues to act out in Mr. Welch's class. Andrea feels confused about why she can't seem to control her behavior and feels all alone because her mom is mad at her. She doesn't know whom to turn to. That night she plays too roughly with her little sister and gets in trouble again. She wonders, "Why can't I be good like my sister? No one gets mad at her. I guess I just can't do anything right."

In the dialogue above, you can see how apologizing for your child's behavior sets in motion a vicious circle that affects the whole family. Ms. Jones feels bad about herself and so does Andrea. They get pushed farther and farther apart as they both conclude that they're failures. Andrea is frustrated that her mom doesn't support her, and Ms. Jones is frustrated that Andrea can't control her behavior. Both feel increasingly helpless.

As you can see from these two vignettes, becoming an advocate for your child gives you the potential to change the environment she experiences at school and, in so doing, reduce her bad feelings and thus the bad behavior she exhibits in response. By reframing your child's behaviors and traits, you may enlist teachers to shift their perspective and try out strategies that are less discouraging to your child.

Similarly, in addition to enhancing your relationship with her, you will improve her self-esteem just by becoming an advocate. Children internalize their parents' attitudes toward them. When you show your child that you are willing to go out on a limb to defend her, she knows she is worthwhile and will be more likely to work hard to demonstrate to you and her teachers that you are right in defending her. She will feel safe, protected, and loved. All of these lead to feelings of self-worth and a determination to do the best she can.

CONSTRUCTING GOOD BEHAVIOR

One of the most effective ways to encourage good behavior in your child is to continually construct interpretations that her existing behavior is already good behavior. Or you can at least identify ways in which her behavior is meaningful or makes sense in some way. For example, in the case of Andrea and Mr. Welch, the parent suggested to the teacher that her daughter's behavior was simply an effort to maintain newfound friendships rather than a pernicious symptom of ADHD. This ability to interpret your child's behavior as having a nonpathological meaning will serve her in many ways and will improve your relationship with her. In some ways, more than anything else in the world, that is what your child wants and needs—for you to be on her side.

As you demonstrate that you are her advocate, your child will internalize the ability to reframe her self-understanding in positive ways. This ability is the basis of self-esteem. In addition, she will internalize the ability to defend and protect herself. This skill will serve her in two ways: first, she will be able to soothe herself; second, she'll be able to stand up for herself. These abilities will become a foundation of her ability to create positive mood states and to change her internal state in the face of negative feedback.

The following exercise will encourage you to search for positive explanations for your child's behavior, which will in turn help you become an articulate advocate for your child. It will also help you to teach your child how to do this for herself. This practice becomes very important, because the diagnosis of ADHD has a tendency to make all of the child's behavior seem to others like it is a result of the disorder. In fact, much of your child's behavior may not be related to the diagnosis of ADHD at all. And even the behavior that is related to this difference can be reframed to show how it represents a gift.

EXERCISE: Storytelling

Spend a week observing your own reactions to your child's behavior or to reports of her behavior from school. During this week, keep a journal of these reactions and thoughts. Write down the behavior that you observed or what the teacher said about your child. Then record the story that you tell yourself about your child. For example, perhaps Mrs. Dugan, your daughter Janet's teacher, calls to tell you that your daughter seems to be daydreaming throughout much of class and, when she's called on, makes it clear that she wasn't paying attention. Write down what the teacher tells you, then record your thoughts about what you've heard. So, in this example, you'd write, "When Mrs. Dugan told me about Janet's daydreaming in class, I felt frustrated with her. Why can't she just pay attention like all the other kids? Maybe she isn't as smart as the other kids. Maybe her ADHD is a progressive disorder and she's going to continue to get worse. She might fail a grade or just drop out of school when she's sixteen. How is she going to make it in the world if she can't get good grades in school? She's going to be shut out from all the opportunities for higher education and won't be able to make a career for herself."

After one week of just recording events and your reactions, purposefully change the stories you tell yourself. Search for positive interpretations of your child's behavior. Write down a story that makes your child's behavior meaningful and positive. Create happy endings. It doesn't matter if the stories are true. What we know is that these stories can become self-fulfilling prophecies. So for now just create stories that frame your child in positive ways. For example, when Mrs. Dugan complains about Janet's daydreaming, a good story would be the following: "Today, after Mrs. Dugan called to complain about Janet daydreaming in class, I was really frustrated with Mrs. Dugan. Of course Janet is daydreaming in her class. She is very creative and imaginative. I bet she was so excited about what Mrs. Dugan had been talking about ten minutes earlier that she reflected deeply about the class material and went off on an original, inventive line of thought. Maybe I can teach Janet to share with Mrs. Dugan and the class what she was thinking about the material. Maybe if Janet can share her process, then Mrs. Dugan will gain an appreciation for her curiosity and how reflective and imaginative she is. Someday Janet will make brilliant, creative contributions to whatever field she goes into, because of her powerful imagination."

Ask your child directly what was going on in her mind during the event described by the teacher. Listen carefully to your child. If she offers a meaningful explanation for her behavior, accept it and incorporate it into your story. Keep in mind that often children aren't able to articulate their inner process clearly. They may just feel confused and not have a good understanding of what happened or why it happened. You can offer to your child the positive stories you have generated and see if they seem right to her. You may be surprised to find that your child says, "Yes, that's exactly what happened. I was so flustered by getting in trouble that I forgot that I had been thinking about the material presented earlier in class. How did you know?"

One of the most heartwarming stories I have heard about the power of listening to a child is one told by legendary educator Annemarie Roeper (personal communication). She had been called in to talk with a young boy who consistently showed behavior problems. Her primary strategy was to listen and inquire rather than lecture. After a lengthy discussion, she asked, "But why do these problems keep happening after we have these conversations?" The young boy answered, "But, Mrs. Roeper, this is the first time I've ever grown up!" This story reveals to us that each child is struggling to do her best, as she goes through the challenges of growing up in a changing body in a changing world, facing many difficult challenges in mind, body, emotion, and spirit.

EXERCISE: The Apple Doesn't Fall Far from the Tree

One way to help yourself to generate positive stories for your child is to explore ways in which your behavior has been similar to hers. Through the power of nature or nurture, there are very likely some similarities between your child's "bad" behavior and your own ways of being in the world. This might be tough for you, especially if you have worked hard to overcome a tendency to goof off, act out, or rebel and have moved in the opposite direction by becoming overly controlled. Or perhaps it's obvious how much like your child you are, but you have exerted enormous discipline to overcome your own difficulties in paying attention or behaving appropriately. It can be painful to admit that those difficulties are part of who you are. Even if you feel as if you're the opposite of your child, try to recall times when you acted in ways that were similar to the behavior that gets your child in trouble.

Assign yourself a half hour a day for one week just to think about how you are like your child. In your journal, write down specific memories of events in which you acted like your child or got in trouble in the same way your child gets in trouble. For example, maybe you remember that your freshman year in college you failed two classes because you just weren't interested in your studies and wanted to explore your newfound independence. Maybe you recall a time you got in trouble at school because you insulted another student. Think about why you did what got you in trouble, and try to understand it. Reflect on how you understood it at that time compared to how you understand it now. One parent remembered being dragged to the principal's office in sixth grade for having hit another student. She remembered being mystified about why she had done this. She couldn't explain to herself or the principal why she had hit the student. As the parent remembered this incident, she realized that she had just experienced significant losses in her family at the time she got in trouble. She realized that no one had talked to her about how she was feeling and that she must have been taking it out on this other student at school. Of course, when she was in sixth grade she could not explain her actions, but as an adult she saw that it was obvious why it had happened.

Write in your journal your own reflections about behaviors you share or have shared in your past with your child. Try to see how the reasons behind your own behavior may be similar to those that explain your child's behavior. For example, the mother who remembered hitting another student realized that maybe her daughter had some feelings of loss around the fact that her husband had recently lost his job and seemed depressed. She saw that maybe her daughter needed to talk about the dramatic changes in the family.

Take action on any insights that emerge. For example, talk to your child about any recent losses or stresses in the family. Make sure she has a chance to talk about any feelings of sadness, anger, or fear that she may be feeling in response to these events in the family. Your child is very sensitive, and you may have felt that by not talking about recent stressors you were protecting your child. However, children will often be even more anxious when there is silence around significant changes. The more open you can be in talking about your own feelings and reactions, the more your child will benefit, even if your own reactions are negative. Your child will feel connected to you only if you genuinely share your reactions. Because children diagnosed with ADHD are particularly sensitive to when people are being insincere, your child will be disturbed by any perception that you're not being straight with her, and she will tend to think that things are worse than they really are. For example, if the mother in the previous example shares with her child that she is worried about Dad and that they both have some anxieties about his job loss, her child will actually feel relieved and more connected to her. The daughter probably sensed the tension all along, and now she will have validation of these feelings and also a chance to share her own anxieties. Of course, you want to be both honest and protective.

This means revealing your fears, sadness, and anger but also reassuring your child that many resources are available and that while this is a difficult time, you are certain to make it through.

If it seems appropriate, you should share with your child your own previous life experiences that are similar to what she is going through. This will help you to connect with your child and show her how one can overcome difficulties. You should also share what you did to turn your situation around or what you wish you had done to turn things around sooner. These stories will help your child feel less alone and more supported, and that will help her get through difficult times.

SUMMARY

In this chapter, we discussed the fact that what your child wants and needs more than anything in the world is a close connection to you. Your child's relationship with you will be the cornerstone of her efforts to turn her problems into strengths.

CHAPTER 5

The Gift of Creativity

In this chapter we begin our exploration of the five gifts of ADHD, starting with the gift of creativity. We will review how your child's spaciness, distractibility, and impulsiveness are essential attributes for promoting creativity. Fire needs oxygen to shine and burn. Similarly, creative genius or inspiration requires a certain sort of openness—exactly the sort of openness your child displays. Creativity often requires reframing or rethinking old problems. Openness (sometimes given the more negative name "spaciness") provides a larger frame for seeing a bigger picture, allowing for space to solve old problems. Many people have said that the definition of *insanity* is doing the same thing repeatedly but expecting different results. Spaciness lends itself to achieving a different level of thought from that which typically creates most problems. Thus, children with ADHD who have been labeled as spacey often have the capacity to solve problems created by rigid modes of thinking. Daydreaming is the font of creativity—it is essentially the process of engaging the imagination.

Imagination creates dreams of possibilities. In a review of the emerging research on the benefits of daydreaming, author Josie Glausiusz concludes that "daydreaming, far from being a total time-waster, is a potential portal to the Nobel Prize—as it was for Albert Einstein, whose visionary daydreams helped him conceive the theory of relativity while he toiled away at a humdrum job in the Swiss patent office" (2009, 86). Other research supports many benefits of daydreaming. Daydreaming can increase social and emotional intelligence. We can release troublesome emotions safely in our imaginary world rather than in the real one, where the consequences would be problematic. And in our imagination we can rehearse social interactions, leading to greater intimacy and more mature relationships (Glausiusz 2009).

SEEING THE BIG PICTURE

Children with ADHD are excellent at seeing the big picture, in and out of the classroom. They may miss the little details, but they are often masters at understanding the importance and meaning of academic material. For example, children with ADHD may be struck with wonder and awe at the miraculous workings of nature as they learn about photosynthesis and how plants take in sunlight to grow. They may wonder what happens in cloud-covered regions of the world and start to generate ideas for how to get sunlight to plants on cloudy days. As this example illustrates, children with ADHD are often deeply engaged with material in creative and novel ways. They may not remember the symbols for sodium and potassium on the periodic table of elements, but they are very curious and interested and typically try to come up with solutions to problems in creative ways.

Typical modes of assessment in the academic world require the ability to repeat small details of abstract processes. This is the most difficult way of learning for children with ADHD. There are methods of evaluation in the educational system that acknowledge the startling gifts your child has to offer. The good news is that, if your child can emerge unscathed from his education, he can find a niche in the real world that will reward him highly for his ardent curiosity, creativity, and ability to solve problems in innovative ways.

THE ENERGY OF IMPULSE

To think daringly original thoughts and to create new ideas or perspectives requires impulsiveness. *Impulsiveness* is the urge to do things or think things that are new and daring, that fall outside the boring realm of the everyday. Impulsiveness is the urge to forge ahead into new areas of thought and includes a tendency to be bored with whatever everyone else is doing or thinking. It is a necessary ingredient for forging new ground in any area of study or thought.

Distractibility is the tendency to shift one's attention to thoughts, feelings, or events in the environment that seem to call out to one. A distractible person is the opposite of a horse with blinders on, plodding along carefully in the path determined by his master. People who are distractable have trouble focusing, because they are enchanted with other aspects of their experience. Distractibility is also an essential aspect of creativity, which often manifests in the mixing together of ideas from apparently different and separate domains. In Thom Hartmann's (1997) book *Attention Deficit Disorder: A Different Perception*, he describes how Thomas Alva Edison, who invented the lightbulb and many other things, was characterized by an easy distractibility. He was known to have forty different inventions in progress at one time. He would work on one until he got bored with it and move on to another one as inspiration hit. Another word for distractibility is "flexibility," and it can be put to use in generating groundbreaking innovation and productivity.

The open-minded, distractible spaciness of your child is much like the "beginner's mind" that students of Zen Buddhism purposefully try to cultivate. Your child's way of being is, to some people, a highly sought-after state of mind, achieved only after years of training. The

91

beginner's mind of Zen Buddhism is so important because it allows one to perceive life anew in each moment with freshness and excitement. It lends itself to creativity because, rather than imposing worn-out modes of understanding on the world, the beginner's mind looks at the world in new and fresh ways.

NATURALLY CREATIVE

Your child is truly fortunate to have been given the natural ability to engage in reverie or imaginative thought, to be bold and daring in wanting to bring his imagination into the world, and to be sensitive to inspiration. Despite these gifts, he may struggle in school. This is because, in the early years, traditional educational systems follow a "regurgitation" model. Children are expected to take in material presented in a rigid format and "regurgitate" it back to the teacher, to prove they were listening attentively. This style of learning clashes with the great gifts your child has been given.

However, a naturally creative child who can learn to apply discipline, pay attention to details, and follow through in translating his imaginative flights into completed projects has a huge potential for excellence. And it is much easier to train someone who is creative to be disciplined than it is to teach someone who is focused and disciplined to be creative.

In this chapter, you'll do an exercise to experiment with how impulsiveness can lead to creativity. Then you and your child will have the opportunity to reframe and understand his behavior as creative rather than disordered. You will also work on balancing creativity with respect for others.

EXERCISE: Disciplined Daydreaming

In order for you to gain some empathy for your child, and some understanding of the potential rewards of spaciness and impulsivity, try this exercise. It will guide you to experiment with purposefully adopting these traits. You will want to have your notebook and a pen handy for recording the impact of this experiment. This exercise also includes prescribing a specified daydreaming session for your child. By setting aside a specified time for daydreaming, you show your support for this aspect of his personality while suggesting that if he can limit his daydreaming to this time he may get more out of his school time.

Our culture values hard work and achievement above all else. In our culture, lounging seems almost criminal. With all the demands for chronic self-improvement, who has time for sitting around and spacing out? But what happens to the inner voices calling you or your child to goof off, to lie around all day, or to play? What other people call "laziness" is central to creativity and the discovery and appreciation of life. Genius requires fortuitous insight, imagination, daring originality, and intuition. These are cultivated when you get lost in the corners of your own mind—through play and goofing off.

Opportunities often come from departures from the well-meaning grind. By staying focused, you may miss the genius-making inspiration. With only rational logic and your nose to the grindstone, you can climb higher and higher, but you may never gain the vision that allows you to see where the ladder leads. (Alternatively, by spending all of your free time watching TV or playing video games, you are passively consuming the creative output of other people rather than actively exploring your own inner world.) The exercises in this chapter ask you to indulge your own need to goof off and space out. Remember, this is just an experiment. You may not be able to find the time to allot a half hour a day for the rest of your life, but for one week you should make every effort to cancel unnecessary appointments or commitments and give yourself this opportunity to experience daydreaming.

1. For one week, each day spend a half hour daydreaming. Do not try to solve a specific problem. Do not try to concentrate on one topic. Just let your mind wander wherever it wants to go. Allow

yourself to escape if that is what you feel like doing. Purposely bracket this time off, allowing your mind to take whatever paths it wants to take. Invite in fantasies and daydreams.

2. At the end of the week, write in your journal how this experience has affected you. Where did your mind wander during these times? Your life as a parent is filled with enormous responsibilities and concerns that require focus, discipline, and fortitude. What did this period of reverie feel like for you?

3. Try prescribing your child one half hour a day to daydream as well. Tell him that daydreaming is a wonderful use of imagination that promotes creativity, and so he should do it purposefully for one half hour a day. Invite him to daydream at the same specified time as you, but make sure you each do it alone.

4. Tell your child that, when he is tempted to daydream in school, he should remind himself to save it for the special daydreaming time that you have set aside. Tell him that if he thinks of something important he wants to daydream about during school, he can write it down in his notebook and come back to it during his scheduled daydreaming time. If you join him for one week in this experiment, you can spend some time after your daydreaming sessions to talk about how it felt and what sorts of things you each spent your time thinking about. You will want to emphasize how you value getting lost in imagination.

FEELING GOOD ABOUT FREEING UP TIME

The preceding and following exercises are experiments in escaping, daydreaming, and allowing yourself and your child a break from rational problem solving and effortful striving. You may feel tempted to skip these exercises because you feel that there is no way to make time for them in your schedule and your child's schedule. If you find you cannot possibly set aside the time for these exercises, you may want to review your commitments and see if they are in line with your own values.

For example, are you running your children to multiple commitments each week thinking that each child needs to be involved in a sports activity, an artistic endeavor, and a social event? If so, you might want to give yourself permission to schedule only one organized activity a week for each child. You may feel guilty, but children need unstructured time alone and with their parents and siblings. The symptoms of ADHD may represent a desperate attempt on the part of the child to give his mind the unstructured time it needs to explore. Giving your child this quiet time does him a tremendous service.

Your child needs time away from structured activities for another reason. Many structured activities have an implicit or explicit performance expectation. If your child plays on a sports team, he may feel he has to be good at it or that he is being evaluated and compared to other children. In music disciplines, there is often a sense that children have to master and even excel at the skills involved in the practice. Most organized activities emphasize some form of achievement. If your child is doing poorly in school, these kinds of activities may be a wonderful outlet for him to receive praise in another area, or they may be just another setting in which he has to prove himself. The more activities he is engaged in, the more intense and relentless is the pressure to perform and achieve. This pressure can take its toll on anyone—especially a young child. And it can negatively affect a child diagnosed with ADHD even more intensely. Children with ADHD have a strong need for unstructured time to nurture their creativity. Creativity requires free time to explore, to play, and to pretend. If much of your child's time is being shaped by structured activities, he will be restless and disruptive. He needs and prefers the time to explore and create his own structure. This is not to say that children should not participate in any extracurricular activities—just that they need fewer. To start, set the guideline that each child in your family gets to participate in one activity per week. If the soccer season lasts for four months, then that is the only activity for that child during that time period. Try this as an experiment and see how you, your spouse, and your children respond.

Similarly, parents need their own downtime and personal lives. If you are spending all of your free time running your children to their commitments, you're not taking good care of yourself. Your marriage needs time for you and your spouse to have adult conversation. If you are single, your romantic life needs you to have energy to spend in connecting with other people. Don't feel guilty for taking time away from your children to focus on your love life. Parents who are happily in love will find it easier to be better parents. Taking care of children, particularly those diagnosed with ADHD, takes an enormous amount of energy, and the energy generated by a fulfilling connection to a romantic partner can be an important resource for you as a parent. If you spend all of your time taking care of your child, you will soon find yourself depleted, and you, your child, and your partner will suffer.

EXERCISE: Fulfill Your Urges

This exercise will have one component for parents to try and one for the child to try. You the parent will benefit from this exercise by becoming more sensitive to your own impulses, which will create a better understanding of your child's impulsiveness. Loosening up may help your child in another way. Sometimes, the more rigid parents are in controlling their own impulses, the more impulsive their children are. This is similar to the cliché that the pastor's kids will always be the most rebellious. In her book *Awakening Intuition*, Dr. Mona Schultz links ADHD to intuition and the tendency to act out unexpressed impulses in the family. She writes that "children with ADD often unconsciously act out any turmoil at home. Mom and Dad fight, then try to smooth the matter over. But Junior trips over the carpet and acts it out physically" (1999, 330). While her example relates to unexpressed tensions, it is also true of unexpressed energies, inclinations, and impulses. For example, if you are overly restrained and never allow yourself to give voice to any irreverent comments, you may find your child blurting out inappropriate comments everywhere you go.

Reserve a whole or half day in which you can spend the time following your own urges. During this time, if you want to watch TV all day, do that. If you want to go to the woods and walk around and then eat a hot fudge sundae, then let yourself do that. If you want to sleep most of the time, do that. Allow yourself to closely follow your urges. If some of your impulses are not appropriate to act on, let yourself explore mentally instead. Ask yourself, "What is underlying this urge? Is there some way I can honor it?" For example, maybe you feel an urge to call a friend and tell him off. Spend some time thinking about what you would really like to communicate to this friend. Think of how you could communicate your needs to this friend in a way that is not explosively angry. Follow through and take action based on this realization.

Write in your journal about how this made you feel. What did you do? How did you feel, allowing yourself to indulge your own urges and impulses? Did you learn something new about yourself? Use this experience to help you connect with your child for the next part of the exercise.

If your child is between five and nine years old, tell him you want to talk to him about the "Urge Monster." If he is older, you can talk more straightforwardly about uncontrollable urges. You can share with him some of your own urges as an example. Tell your child that everyone has an Urge Monster and that it is important to feed the monster but to not let it control you. Ask your child to talk about some of his urges, and then brainstorm with him to find ways to feed and control the Urge Monster without getting into trouble. Here is an example of how this might go:

Dad: Remember when I talked with your teacher about how you were disrupting art class by jumping around and telling everyone that you were going to have a baby sister? Sometimes we all get urges to do things like that, where we want to stir things up and blurt out what we really feel. Just today, I thought I'd like to tell my boss to just leave me alone when she was in a hurry for me to finish my work. But I realized my boss might get mad at me if I told her what I really thought. And I know that sometimes the Urge Monster just needs to be fed a little bit, and it will quiet down. So I called your mommy on the phone and told her what I really thought about my boss. Then I calmed down and could talk to my boss about what I thought was a more reasonable time frame for me to get my work done, and she agreed with me. How could you learn to feed the Urge Monster?

Sandy: I was just so excited about Samantha in Mommy's belly, and I wanted to tell everybody how good I felt about it. There was no way I could stay quiet.

Dad: How could you feed the urge without disrupting the class? Maybe you could draw a picture of the Urge Monster, or draw a picture for your sister when she arrives?

Sandy: Yeah, I bet I could tell the monster that I could wait and tell Daddy how I'm so excited for my sister to get here. And I could draw a picture for my new sister to hang in her bedroom.

Dad: That's a great idea. Sometimes just promising yourself that you will tell someone else will help you keep quiet when the teacher wants you to sit still.

The same urges that cause problems can also be seen as creative urges for self-expression. By learning to feed urges through creative expression, your child can learn to both honor his impulses and channel those urges in creative ways. Creativity is often experienced as an urge to create. When all impulses are suppressed, creativity often gets suppressed, too. Being connected to your impulses and urges is important for both you and your child. For your child diagnosed with ADHD, connecting with his impulses allows him to utilize one of his wonderful gifts—creativity. When creativity is combined with discipline, your child has the potential to be a superstar.

REFRAMING SYMPTOMS: FINDING CREATIVITY

When a parent does not pay careful attention to a child's inner process, it is easy to miss his creativity in everyday life. While the teacher complains that he is spacing out during her presentation on the structure of our government, your child may be generating possible solutions for eliminating wasteful governmental spending. While your child appears to be trying to get out of going to his music lessons, he may be singing Broadway show tunes in his mind, with perfect tempo and remembering all the words. As you can see, if a child isn't doing what he's supposed to be doing, we commonly think he is misbehaving. In fact, he may be exploring and expressing his own unique gifts that do not match up with society's tight schedules and plans for him.

In fact, what adults often think of as goofing off can be one of the most important activities for any child, but particularly for a creative child. If your child is diagnosed with ADHD, you may recognize that he does not have the same attention span and sustained focusing abilities of other children, but you must also acknowledge his superior creativity that, as a parent, you are entrusted with nourishing and nurturing. But you cannot nurture his creativity by getting him to conform to the demands of traditional ideas of achievement. You nurture his creativity by making allowances for his differences and unstructuring his life accordingly.

Goofing Off Is Not Giving Up

Let's examine this idea of goofing off. Creativity requires goofing off. Goofing off is play, experimentation, and trying out new ideas— then adjusting them to see what fits, what works, and what is more fun. As a parent, you may have observed your child engaging in an activity for a small amount of time and then starting to goof off. For example, one parent complained that her daughter asked to take lessons to learn to play the clarinet. She would practice her lessons at home for only fifteen minutes, and then she would put her clarinet down and dance wildly, running around the house like a Tasmanian devil. Her mother considered this giving up, feeling frustrated at how much it cost to buy the clarinet and pay for lessons and thinking that the money was being wasted. But it can also be viewed as another form of creativity, or a strategy for discharging all of her excitement about playing music. It might be her boredom with practicing lessons, which contrasts with her desire to add her own daring and impulsive energy to the practice of the clarinet. So goofing off is not giving up. In reframing this behavior as a form of creativity, we can help the child's wild energy to be channeled into creative musical abilities.

Music coach and psychologist Dr. Lane Arye has written in his book *Unintentional Music: Releasing Your Deepest Creativity* (2001) about how goofing off can feed one's deepest creativity. As an example, he describes a music lesson with a classical guitarist in which the teacher asked a student to amplify a particular hand gesture that was irrelevant to the music being played. The student amplified his gesture until he was making wild body movements and screaming with delight. The teacher writes that, after the apparent derailment of the music lesson, "I asked him whether he could express this ecstatic wildness in his music. Franz grabbed his guitar and played the same piece as before. But this time he played it with incredible energy... He said, with an irrepressible smile, that he had never thought it was allowable to play like that" (Arye 2001, 109). This interaction can be viewed as a model for parents interacting with their children diagnosed with ADHD. You can become a detective and search for ways in which your child's apparent "symptoms" represent creativity or could be channeled to enhance your child's creative expression.

On the Importance of Being Confused

Similarly, let's look at confusion. Your child may get into trouble in school for looking or acting confused when called on or when participating in classroom exercises. His confusion or apparent disorientation may give the impression that he is not paying any attention at all. It may make him look less intelligent and provoke harsh comments from teachers and students alike. However, this sense of confusion can be reframed as reflecting a higher intellectual sophistication, because it can result from an appreciation of the deeper complexity of the topic. It can be looked at as an appreciation of the mysterious, as an expression of humility in the face of the complexity of the world.

Confusion is an admission that one does not fully understand the material being covered. And creativity requires that a person acknowledge that there is a deeper aspect of what is being presented. Therefore, confusion can also be thought to be a necessary component of creativity. Confusion can represent an experience of the mystery of what is being taught. For example, in reflecting on photosynthesis, a child with ADHD might be awed by the order and harmony in the universe that allows for the sun to nurture plant growth, which in turn nurtures the human environment. But that same child might get derailed by the experience of awe and get confused about the detailed aspects of the biology of photosynthesis. In fact, the constructed explanations offered to students by teachers are often oversimplifications. In pretending to know it all, students and teachers gloss over the complexity and mystery of the world.

Confusion, though it is essential to creativity, gets a bad rap in our culture, which makes a virtue of being sharp and quick at all times. These cultural demands overlook the value of being slow and uncomprehending. But admitting or experiencing not knowing can be liberating. In fact, the struggle to always have the right answer actually prevents a person from learning. If we think we have the answers, or if we are seeking only one answer, then we are not open to a deeper understanding or to exploring other ways of seeing the world.

EXERCISE: The Creativity of Everyday Life

In this exercise you will be asked to practice reframing your child's symptoms as manifestations of creativity. You will be asked to search for ways in which his behavior can be seen as acting or thinking outside the box. In addition, you will be guided to find ways to honor your child's expression rather than suppress it, and you will ask your child to practice becoming aware of his creativity.

1. Start out by becoming aware of a symptom your child demonstrates. A typical complaint about children with a diagnosis of ADHD is that they don't follow directions very well. Let's say that when you ask your son to keep quiet in church, he often seems to become defiant and will burst out with irreverent comments that the whole congregation can hear. You interpret this behavior as purposefully defiant and rebuke the child with harsh words and threats of dire consequences if he does not keep quiet. In response, his behavior escalates, setting a vicious circle in motion.

2. Generate possible positive explanations regarding how this behavior is creative. For example, maybe your son is trying to make the church services more lively. You might commend him for trying to participate or make a contribution in his own way. Perhaps your son's irreverence reflects a need for something that is more down to earth and relevant to the concerns of the parishioners.

3. Engage in a discussion with your child, asking him to reflect on his behavior. Listen while remaining open to a nonantagonistic understanding of his behavior. For example, you can calmly ask him why he is contributing to the church service in this way when he was asked to keep quiet. Listen attentively to how your son understands his behavior. He may surprise you by saying that he noticed that people laugh when he makes these outbursts, and he wants people to laugh more at church to show how happy they are to be there. He might tell you that maybe people would come more often if they laughed at church. This is a radically different interpretation of his behavior, and it gives you the opportunity to see it as sweet generosity rather than defiance related to ADHD.

4. Give your child praise for his creativity and tell him that this is an example of his ability to think and act in ways that are outside the box. You might also commend him on his perception of the problems—for example, with the church service—and his efforts at solving the problems. Remember, creativity means that, rather than mastering and following what other people are doing, your child questions the way things are done and finds ways of doing things differently.

5. Tell your child that, while you appreciate his creativity and think he has a lot to offer, he needs to be aware that some people might be disturbed by his outbursts and see his behavior as disrespectful. You can explain that while his behavior demonstrates his gifts, he needs to balance his creative expression with respect for other people.

6. Engage his creativity by helping him to devise ways to express himself while still being respectful to everyone else. Spend some time brainstorming ideas together. For example, you could suggest to the minister that, rather than having a stuffy choir every week, they could have a jazz band play renditions of some of the hymns. Maybe your son could think of inoffensive jokes

to tell members of the church during the social hour. Maybe he could paint a picture of people laughing in church and give it to the minister.

Having completed this practice of reframing, communicating, and problem solving with your child, you will be well on your way to increasing your connection. By trying to not become frustrated and assume the worst about his behavior, you demonstrate an enormous amount of respect for him. You will also find that, by listening to his motivations rather than assuming the worst, you gain an increased appreciation for his creativity and positive motivations; the common reaction of frustration and threats is transformed into increased intimacy. As you change your perceptions, you also transform your child's perceptions of himself. As these ideas change, behavior will follow. You are well on your way to transforming your child's problems into strengths!

EXERCISE: Fill In the Blank

One of the easiest ways to generate positive interpretations of your child's behavior is to purposefully look for them. For the following exercise, you will write the sentence stems shown below on a piece of lined paper or on a page in your notebook and ask your child to fill in the blanks. This can be fun for him because it asks him to use his creativity and gives him a chance to show you what he's really thinking.

1. I am most creative when _____.

2. I can show others my imagination by _____.

3. I am really good at _____.

4. My last really good idea was _____.

5. The last idea I had about something that needed to be improved was _____ .

6. One thing I do differently from everyone else is _____ .

7. I do this my way because _____ .

8. I can help others because _____ .

9. I can make the world a better place because _____ .

10. The thing I like most about myself is _____ .

11. Other people like me because _____ .

12. I wish people would understand that _____ .

13. I wish I could show people _____ .

14. I wish my teacher knew _____ .

15. I wish my parents knew _____ .

When you have completed these sentences with your child, you can collaborate on translating some of the results into action. For example, in the case where the child thinks that church needs to be more fun, you can take his comments seriously and suggest that you and he talk with the minister. If you agree that the church is too dull, maybe you could try another church. Perhaps you could give him a chance to show the family how he would create a sermon or service that would be more fun. Once your child's impulse is honored or given expression, you can expect his problematic behavioral expression of it to be reduced.

Let Your Child Contribute

Another reason for honoring your child's impulses is that very often he truly does have something to offer. Sometimes children with ADHD are expressing what a lot of other people really think but are too controlled to say. Thom Hartmann (1997), an author and advocate for understanding ADHD as a gift, has argued that the ways in which children diagnosed with ADHD disrupt classes are signs that our educational system needs to change. If your child insists that classes are boring, he may be right.

Dr. Lane Arye writes, "Old-fashioned ideas about music pedagogy are symptomatic of a larger societal pattern. Both rank and privilege are bestowed on those who are older, better educated, professional, successful. A mere child or someone in a lower socioeconomic position is often forced to humble herself, hold herself back, keep her good ideas hidden, and follow those who have more assigned power... Being deeply democratic would mean giving the student a say in this process, letting her in on the decisions that affect her education... For if the needs and ideas of students were taken into consideration, then much of the rebellion that is a normal part of education would be seen as creativity and used to further the teaching process" (2001, 132).

The educational system could benefit from providing more opportunities for creativity, less focus on obedience, more opportunities for fully engaging students' senses rather than just their minds, and more attention to students' individual needs and aptitudes. Not only would such an approach honor the child by reframing his behavior as creative, but it would also allow respect for the child's impulse to transform structures that are not working and are in need of change.

SUMMARY

This chapter reframed the ADHD symptoms of distractibility, daydreaming, and impulsiveness as creativity. Children with ADHD are gifted in imagination and original thought. Specific exercises and strategies were recommended for discovering ways in which so-called symptoms are actually signs of creativity.

CHAPTER 6

Showing the Way: Ecological Consciousness

Children with the diagnosis of ADHD have a preference for learning about the world through hands-on engagement. They like to be immersed in the topics they are learning about. They are often very curious about the natural and organic world, feeling a deep connection to it. This gift for engaged, experiential learning is often overlooked because existing educational systems focus on abstract learning and rote memorization. What looks like a disorder can be viewed as a poor match between a style of learning and current standards of teaching.

Not only do children with a diagnosis of ADHD learn through engagement, they have an ardent curiosity about the living, breathing organic world. They often feel connected with and attuned to nature and animals. As a result, they may represent a much-needed force in the world: protecting the environment.

In chapter 1, we discussed how anything different from normal is often labeled "disorder" by psychologists, psychiatrists, and teachers. However, in order to argue that different from normal is bad, one has to believe that normal is good and healthy. In contrast, if one looks at the state of the environment, one might argue that climate change, for example, is the result of "normal" modes of consciousness—the idea that nature is exploitable and expendable. Your child's difference may be, in some ways, better than normal, because she may become one who guides us toward a healthier relationship with our environment.

WHAT IS ECOLOGICAL CONSCIOUSNESS?

An ecological consciousness is a way of being that respects the natural world—plants, trees, animals, and insects. Individuals with this form of intelligence feel directly related to and engaged with the natural world. Children with an ecological consciousness often are very sensitive to animals and ardently interested in nature. These children like to spend time outside, doing anything from picking flowers and leaves and examining worms and insects in the dirt to simply rambling.

Howard Gardner described naturalist intelligence as a separate type of intelligence uniquely capable of solving problems related to the natural world (1999). He discussed Darwin as an exemplar of this type of intelligence, a person who was intensely interested in understanding the natural world and who spent his life directly engaged with the natural world.

Nature as Medicine

When the first edition of The Gift of ADHD (2005) was released, many of the ideas presented in it were embraced and featured in mainstream media—except for the idea of ecological intelligence. In some places this idea was received as "California-speak." Ironically, even then it was one of the most scientifically validated interventions for increasing attention. The research robustly demonstrates the positive impact of time spent in nature on attention in general and ADHD specifically.

Since the release of the first edition, the idea of nature as medicine has gone mainstream. The National Wildlife Federation has formed the national coalition "No Child Left Inside." This coalition advocates for legislation and other national initiatives to address the crisis of children's disconnect from nature as TV, computers, and other digital media increasingly consume children's lives. The need for this effort is a clear sign that something has gone wrong in our culture. One or two generations ago, children played outside until dusk, dreading the call to come inside for dinner and bedtime. Now we need public service announcements telling us about the health benefits of playing outside and prescribing a recommended daily dose of outside time.

Richard Louv's book *Last Child in the Woods: Saving Our Children from Nature-Deficit Disorder* (2005) became a national best seller, and by 2009 *Time* magazine was declaring ecological intelligence to be one of "ten ideas changing the world right now" (Walsh 2009, 66). Daniel Goleman's book *Ecological Intelligence* (2009) describes the need for the development of ecological intelligence as the solution to many global crises. The World Future Society ranked nature deficit disorder as the fifth most important trend that would shape 2007 and the world to come (Charles et al. 2008).

The No Child Left Inside coalition is not the only organization aiming to reconnect kids with nature. Others include the Children and Nature Network and the National Forum on Children and Nature, hosted by the Conservation Fund. These organizations seek to address the growing concerns about the possible consequences of a "nature-deficit disorder" as coined by Louv.

As is the case with any new idea going mainstream, there are those who are at the forefront. These leaders are showing us what happens when we take ecological intelligence seriously. Teton Science Schools, for example, has taken the momentum of ecological intelligence and run with it. Teton Science Schools in Jackson Hole, Wyoming, has been fulfilling its mission of connecting people, nature, place, and education since 1967 (personal communication, Teton Science Schools, 2009). The school not only nurtures ecological intelligence but rightly views it as a possible cure for many childhood health issues such as obesity, ADHD, and depression. In this program, children experience the intimacy of connection to people and a place that forges a community—in sharp contrast to the experience of many children who spend large amounts of time watching TV and playing video games. This school gives us a sense of what education and child rearing will look like if we act to change our increasingly technology-centered world.

Not only has the idea of ecological intelligence spread like wildfire, but, as mentioned above, scientific research is also increasingly showing that time in nature has direct and measurable positive effects on attention (Berman, Jonides, and Kaplan 2008). Stephen Kaplan proposed the attention restoration theory, explaining that time spent in nature offers a relief from directed attention and thereby restores our capacity to pay attention. Research has shown improvements in focused attention following time spent in natural settings, including sitting in gardens, walking in the park, or even gazing at artwork depicting natural beauty. So many studies have shown positive results that one review of the literature describes time spent in nature as a recommended healing method—a readily available therapy with no side effects and zero cost that consistently and reliably boosts cognitive functioning (Berman, Jonides, and Kaplan 2008).

While many children would benefit from spending more time in

> When asked what they are paying attention to in class, children with ADHD often remark that they are looking out the window. They are deeply engaged in observing the trees, birds, or any glimpse of wildlife the window opens up for the child. Often these children are caught by what Abram calls "the spell of the sensuous."

nature, it is true that kids with ADHD may have an intrinsic need to spend more time in nature and are therefore doubly injured by these cultural trends. Kids with ADHD usually don't want to sit in a class learning about nature—they want to learn actively, in the natural world. Whereas current education systems demand focused concentration on abstract concepts, children with ADHD may be gifted with what author David Abram calls "sensuous consciousness" (1996).

The Spell of the Sensuous

David Abram (1996) writes in his book *The Spell of the Sensuous* about the devastating impact of our disengagement from the natural, organic world we live in. He depicts a culture that has become so absorbed in its own intellectualized abstractions, supported by increasingly sophisticated technologies, that we have become numb to the destruction of our environment. Abram (1996, 272) refuses to put forth any utopian solutions to the problems he poses, suggesting that such ideas would themselves invite attention away from our sensuous surroundings:

> A genuinely ecological approach does not work to attain a mentally envisioned future, but strives to enter, ever more deeply, into the sensorial present. It strives to become ever more awake to the other lives, the forms of sentience and sensibility that surround us in the open field of the present moment.

Abram's ideas offer one avenue for understanding the gifts that our culture calls an attention deficit—the style of consciousness that gets called ADHD is precisely what is necessary to reverse the environmental damage wrought by the dulling of our senses. For example, when asked what they are paying attention to in class, children with ADHD often remark that they are looking out the window. They are deeply engaged in observing the trees, birds, or any glimpse of wildlife the window opens up for the child. Often these children are caught by what Abram calls "the spell of the sensuous." Under such a spell, the child perceives the concrete, everyday world as almost magical, whereas the abstract world of thoughts and books is not compelling. Abram argues that this is a positive quality and entails being enchanted by the world of the senses, often linked to organic natural events.

A student named Mike reported that, rather than listening to what was going on in class, he would find himself drawn to watching the way the sun reflected off the leaves of the trees outside the class window, the way the wind blew through the leaves, and the way the squirrels played among the branches. He found himself asking why leaves are green and how the squirrels lived off of the tree. From the teacher's standpoint, this behavior looked like a failure to pay attention to the classroom tasks required for success in school. However, Mike's apparent disengagement was actually engagement with the small natural landscape available to him through the window of the classroom. Mike's interest in the tree represented not a deficit disorder or a lack of intrinsic curiosity but an attunement to the natural world. His questioning about what was inside the trees and interest in why the leaves were green reflected a sophisticated curiosity about the world around him, which was quite advanced for his grade level. He was interested in questions that would not be addressed until much later. He would have to wait until high school biology classes to learn about the mechanism of photosynthesis and the greenness of leaves. It may have been that his difficulties in school resulted from his curiosity far outpacing the studies of his grade level, which required him to contend with the mechanics of reading and writing rather than nourish his ardent curiosity about the world around him. Unfortunately, by the time he reached high school he had had so many experiences of failure that the questions that had originally interested him receded in the background, overshadowed by his chronically negative academic evaluations.

Abram suggests that modern culture has turned its attention to written text. The abstraction and intellectualization of the modern consciousness has led to participation not in the world surrounding us but in the books and texts that tell us about that very world. In depicting the modern evolution of consciousness, from which ADHD is a deviation, Abram writes, "it is only when a culture shifts its participation to these printed letters that the stones fall silent. Only as our senses transfer their animating magic to the written word do the trees become mute, the other animals dumb" (1996, 131). For Mike, the trees and animals were alive; it was the book that was dead. To Abram, Mike's attention to the spell of the sensuous would not be seen as regressive but could in fact show a way of being in the world that would facilitate an ecological mind-set. In Abram's words, "it is only at the scale of our direct, sensory interactions with the land around us that we can appropriately notice and respond to the immediate needs of the living world" (1996, 268).

If an "attention deficit" represents an increased sensitivity to the wider community of nature, then this style of consciousness is one that needs to be cultivated in order to preserve our environment—not dulled through medication. After all, it is the dulled modern style of consciousness that has led to the growing ecological crisis our culture faces. Daniel Goleman (2009), in his book *Ecological Intelligence*, similarly suggests that sensitivity to the impact of our behavior on the environment is one of many types of intelligence that should be highly valued, on par with the intelligence measured by standardized tests.

A TALE OF TWO STUDENTS

Although ADHD can represent a form of environmental intelligence with many gifts to offer, you are familiar with how this gift can play out negatively in the classroom. Below are brief characterizations of two students, one with "normal" modes of paying attention (Sam) and one with an ecologically engaged consciousness (John).

Sam is sitting quietly in science class. He is focused intently on what the teacher is saying about the structure of flowers. Some of the information is familiar from Sam's reading in the textbook. Sam wants to pay careful attention to what the teacher says because he

113

knows there will be a quiz soon on the anatomy of a flower.
He wants to do well on the quiz.

John is having a hard time staying in his seat. The teacher is
droning on and on about something, but John is mesmerized by
the scene from his classroom window. He's watching the rain
fall on the plants and trees near the fence across the street. John
wonders if the plants and trees drink the water and why they
don't get soggy. He wonders if all the insects get washed off the
plants and trees and if they need to drink water from the rain.
John hasn't kept up with his reading because the book seemed
really boring. When he tried to do his homework the night before,
he was too busy watching the neighbor's dog chase squirrels to
focus on the text.

As you can see from these two vignettes, both students are paying attention—just to different things. One student pays attention to books, teachers, and the importance of getting good grades; he remembers that there will be a quiz on the material and this motivates him to pay attention. The other student pays attention to trees, leaves, and animals; he shows ardent curiosity about the world around him. Both are curious and smart, but Sam will likely succeed in school, and John will probably do poorly. Despite his deep intelligence, John's failure in school will likely lead him to believe that he's not smart. He may begin to believe that he just doesn't measure up and will never succeed, so he'll give up trying. John may begin to think there must be something wrong with him, wondering, "Why do I always fail?"

He may be failing because he is being taught using the wrong strategies. There are many teaching strategies that would better fit John's gift of engagement with the sensual world. For example, if, rather than being assigned reading, John was assigned the task of exploring a garden, observing the flowers, and bringing a flower to class, he might then be interested in paying attention to what is going on in the classroom. Because children with ADHD learn through their senses, anchoring lessons firmly in the sensual world of experience will help them to be more involved in what is happening in the classroom.

As a parent, you can engage your child's interest by encouraging these interests rather than dismissing them as distractions. For example, rather than forcing your child to sit down and read quietly, you can ask the teacher to tell you the topic of study ahead of time and then allow for some time to observe or explore in ways that are related to lesson plans. If you cannot find a way to connect the material with sensual learning, then you might offer an opportunity for nature exploration around the neighborhood to help your child prepare for book learning.

THE IMMEDIATE BENEFITS OF OUTSIDE TIME

A 2001 study found that the symptoms of ADHD were relieved by time spent in nature (Faber-Taylor, Kuo, and Sullivan 2001). The study found that children were better able to concentrate, complete tasks, and follow directions after spending playtime in natural, especially green, settings. Activities such as camping, fishing, or playing soccer outside were examples of time spent in natural settings. The authors suggested that these findings were not explainable merely as a result of the subjects' physical activity. For example, playing basketball in paved surroundings did not result in the improvements in concentration that even passive activities in green settings did. Also, the results could not be attributed to the children's engagement in activities they preferred and were willing to settle down in order to participate in. The researchers found that, while children's preferred activities were watching TV or playing video games, these activities did not improve the ability to concentrate as much as playing in nature did.

Fig. 1. ADD symptoms in children are relieved after spending time in nature. The greener the setting, the more the relief.

The authors explain their findings by suggesting that being in nature facilitates a state of involuntary attention that is effortless and provides a rest from *directed attention*, the capacity to focus narrowly. The authors argue that the use of directed attention is like exercising a muscle, and it results in fatigue. The involuntary attention that is promoted by activity in nature offers the child a rest, allowing her to exert directed attention afterward.

Another explanation that supplements the authors' findings is that children with ADHD have a particular attunement to nature and that feeding this need helps them to settle down. So, in some ways, children with this diagnosis need to be connected to nature and are unsettled until this need is met.

Further research support for the power of nature was found in a study of at-risk inner-city girls. The study found that the greener the view from a girl's home (meaning the more nature was visible from a window), the more that girl was able to concentrate, inhibit impulses, and delay gratification (Faber-Taylor, Kuo, and Sullivan 2002). Although this study found this effect only in girls in this sample, the results suggest that when children who have difficulty concentrating stare out classroom windows, they may be attempting to heal themselves. Another study found that students whose dorm rooms had views of nature had greater capacity to sustain attention than students without nature views (Tennessen and Cimprich 1995). Other studies have found physical health benefits to hospital patients whose rooms had views of natural scenery.

These findings indicate a need for a change in how teachers respond to window-gazing. Instead of punishing the child or pointing to the behavior as evidence that she is not trying at all, perhaps it should be permitted for limited amounts of time. In this way, an ADHD child staring out the window can use this intelligent strategy for restoring attention and have a better chance of succeeding.

ENCOURAGING YOUR CHILD'S ATTUNEMENT TO NATURE

Given that your child's way of being in the world and easy connection to nature can be understood as a gift, it may be to her benefit to encourage the development of this talent. It's possible that honoring this gift outside the classroom will allow your child to pay attention inside the classroom.

Behavior Strategies

There are many strategies you can use to honor your child's gift and shape her behavior to achieve greater success in school. One is to never punish your child by taking away her time in nature. Because this time is what she needs to help her concentrate, you would put her in a bind if you were to take away her time in nature as a punishment for not following directions or not doing homework.

Another strategy is to avoid offering time spent in nature as a reward, because it is not effective. It is more helpful to give your child time in nature before she begins her schoolwork than to tell her that if she completes her homework she can then play outdoors. She may very well need her time in nature to facilitate doing her homework. The main idea here is that you want to work with your child's natural gifts rather than against them. By realizing that your child feels a special connection to nature and knowing that this connection is healing for her, you can use playtime in nature as a preparation activity to help her focus, concentrate, and follow through on directions. You may want to create a schedule for your child that involves nature time before homework or household chores.

You can also boost your child's self-esteem in the process of honoring this gift. You can tell her directly that you understand and value the importance of her connection to animals, trees, and the living world. You can also tell her that her engagement with nature is a great gift to offer the world. You can talk about the environmental problems in the world and how they have resulted from the thinking that nature is not as important as human wants and needs. You can tell her how her direct connection to nature represents a different style of being in the world that serves to balance the disregard that can be seen in the normal state of mind. You can also tell her that what the doctors call ADHD is this different style of being, and that it is different from normal, but different in this good way.

Allowing your child to learn in nature is yet another strategy. If you can find a nearby park that has picnic tables, you might choose to allow her to study or read for some amount of time at the park.

Again, this strategy involves going with the flow rather than resisting your child's natural inclination to be in nature.

Project-Based Learning Strategies

One powerful strategy for using your child's engagement with the natural world is to develop and advocate for project-based learning exercises for her, both inside and outside the classroom. This means that in science classes, for example, you try to engage her senses with field trips and exploration of the world.

This type of learning exercise asks children to actually do things rather than just read about them. Children with a diagnosis of ADHD have a hard time processing abstractions or rational, linear representations of the world. However, they can be very effective at solving real-world problems and learning through engagement with the world. As a parent, you can engage your child's interest by introducing her to a project or experience that helps to illuminate a topic she's studying in class. The following exercise is an example that is relevant to science or literature classes. But if you can increase your child's motivation in one topic of interest, and she can demonstrate success in one subject, her self-esteem and self-efficacy will increase, boosting her motivation for other subjects. As she learns that she is capable of succeeding, her enthusiasm will be enhanced and she'll believe that, with effort, she can succeed.

EXERCISE: Creating Your Own Field Trips

Choose one of your child's school subjects that lends itself to spending time in nature, such as science.

Plan and develop a trip or project that will engage your child's senses and is related to your chosen subject. For instance, if your child is learning about animals, plan a trip to the zoo. If she's learning about tree leaves, take a trip to a forest and ask her to pick out some leaves.

Provide praise for your child's energy and ability to follow directions as she participates in the project or exploration. In this way you are validating that she does have the skills to follow directions, focus her energy, and learn new things. You are also validating her creativity and curiosity. When your child's full senses are engaged in learning, her gifts will be evident as she shows a lot of energy, curiosity, and creativity in exploring the world. Reflect back to your child your appreciation of these gifts.

Once you have engaged your child's curiosity, connect her gifts to the lessons being taught in the classroom. Have her think of questions about the topic. Tell her that her school books and teacher can help her find answers to these questions. So, for example, after a trip to a nearby forest to collect leaves, you can direct her to some readings that talk about the structures and function of leaves. In the process, you will channel your child's energy and enthusiasm into finding answers through books and other school resources. This will increase her motivation to participate in the classroom.

You can use the same strategy to help your child with a literature class. You might engage your child's interest by connecting some of the natural elements of a story or book to real-world explorations. For example, if the story takes place near a lake, you can plan a trip to a lake or pond to motivate her to engage with the reading material.

ADVOCATE FOR PROJECT-BASED LEARNING IN SCHOOL

A personal testimony of the value of project-based learning for students with ADHD can be found in the book *Learning Outside the Lines*, written by two students with ADHD who made it through an Ivy League school (Mooney and Cole 2000). These students describe their personal struggle with school and how they overcame their obstacles to succeed in a university setting. They advocate for the use of project-based learning as one way of navigating the educational system. These authors write about how simple changes in the learning environment can make or break academic success: "Only as time went on did simple interventions like the ability to get up out of our seats, the use of a spell checker, and progressive ideas like project-based learning and other modifications to the learning environment allow the pathology to slip into irrelevance and enable us to be successful" (2000, 65).

As a parent, you can become an advocate for these changes on behalf of your child. These same authors talk about having teachers who emphasized spelling and tormented them with bad grades and public humiliation because they couldn't spell. The authors learned to hate school and associate it with personal failure. One of the authors writes about how one teacher, understanding the child's differences, did not penalize the student for poor spelling or emphasize the child's difficulty with spelling. This teacher allowed the student to use a spell-checker, and one of the main struggles of elementary school was ended. This teacher looked for and saw the strengths of the student and emphasized those. These simple changes in the environment can have powerful effects on your child's success and attitude toward school.

If even small changes, like permission to use a spell-checker, can make such a dramatic difference, then you can imagine the benefits of larger changes, such as incorporating project-based learning into your child's coursework. As an advocate for your child, you can meet with each teacher and make them all aware of your child's diagnosis and the importance of project-based learning as an adjunct to regular classroom learning. You can also request that your child's grades be based on projects rather than quizzes or tests.

Each time you advocate for changes in your child's instruction, you should let your child know what you're doing and why you are doing it. In this way, your child will grow to feel that you are on her side and not an antagonist. The power of her feeling that she is supported cannot be overstated. As your child feels that you are advocating for her interests, her motivation to do well in school and to work hard will be increased. In addition, by advocating on her behalf, you are communicating to her that her differences are not deficits, and that she has strengths. Your child will internalize the good feelings that you convey when you advocate for her and when you take action to change the environment rather than just try to change her. As you place some of the blame for her failures on the school environment, you can reverse the self-blame and self-defeating thoughts that have come to plague your child.

An example of what you might say to a teacher follows:

Parent: Mrs. Dugan, I wanted to speak to you about how you can best facilitate my daughter's learning in your class. I have come to see that Janet has a different style of learning. She shows a special engagement with nature and the organic living world and learns best when she is doing and touching and able to get her hands on whatever is being studied. She struggles with details and abstractions, but she is highly curious. I have found that I can increase her motivation for book learning if I tie it to some project or exploration of the organic world. For example, I see you have an upcoming quiz on labeling the parts of a flower. If you can involve the class in looking for real flowers or bring in real flowers and ask them to explore, touch, and develop questions about the flowers, it would be a great help to Janet. I'm not trying to tell you how to teach your class, but I know you have a commitment to reaching each child and engaging each student's interest in science. This is one way that really works with my daughter.

In addition to advocating for project-based learning, you might also want to talk to teachers about strategies of punishment that are likely to fail for your child. It's common for teachers to punish ADHD students for goofing off in class by taking away their recess time. You might want to advocate for your child that recess and time spent out in nature actually help her to concentrate and settle down. Once the teacher takes this away, her behavior is likely to get worse, not better. Sometimes this form of handling behavior leads to a vicious circle. Your child has difficulty sitting still in class, and the teacher says that if she cannot sit in her seat she'll miss recess. Your child gets out of her seat and misses recess, which is her time to connect with nature. In subsequent classes, her behavior gets worse and additional forms of behavioral control and punishment follow, which humiliate your child. All of this makes her feel more negative toward school and more unable to control her own behavior.

Further, consider making the radical suggestion to your child's teacher that, rather than having her recess time taken away, she needs more time for breaks. It may be that instead of ordering time-outs or trips to the principal's office after bad behavior has occurred, the school could implement preventative steps by giving your child small breaks outside in nature before classes.

There is strong reason to believe that playtime in nature would improve all children's educational outcomes. Finland has one of the most highly ranked educational systems, ranking first in literacy and in the top five in math and science. It encourages playtime at regular intervals throughout the school day (Louv 2005). A typical Finnish school day follows a pattern of forty-five minutes of work followed by fifteen minutes of playtime outdoors. Finland's example shows us that we are headed in the wrong direction by creating more performance demands in the classroom and taking away playtime outdoors. It seems clear, from the growing body of research and Finland's example, that time in nature and free play are a basic need of any child and an essential building block of maintaining attention.

Schools and teachers regularly make allowances for children with ADHD. The problem is these allowances are usually stigmatizing or, at the least, do not allow the child to reach her full potential. Students may be taken out of class for remedial help, which may attract the notice and judgment of other students. These interventions may be humiliating and difficult for your child to tolerate. It seems worth advocating for your child's teachers and schools to allow for small nature breaks in place of other forms of remedial intervention.

Similarly, small allowances in the classroom can prevent major outbursts. Simple behavioral interventions like permitting a child to get out of her seat on occasion can go a long way toward making school more tolerable for your child. As a parent, you can ask for behavioral interventions that are not punishing or humiliating for your child and can prevent major interruptions in the classroom.

Jonathan Mooney and David Cole (2000, 70), in *Learning Outside the Lines,* speak to the powerful need for engaging, creative learning strategies:

> Trapped as children by a narrow understanding of what it means to learn, we lost our passion for learning and our passion for school, which we had to fight to regain later in our lives. We also lost the opportunity to develop the intuitive, emotional, and creative parts of our minds. These were identified as irrelevant, as learning became about memorization and sequential thinking, and not about creative, intuitive ideas.

These words may serve as an inspiration for you to ask for changes in your child's learning environment. In so doing, remember that your child's school is already changing the environment to accommodate your child: she may be subjected to frequent time-outs, trips to the principal's office, requirements that she sit in the hallway during recess, remedial interventions, and time out from the regular schedule to take medications. As an advocate, you're simply asking for different accommodations, which will prevent problems by enhancing your child's passion for learning. Instead of punishment, ask for prevention.

MATCHING ENVIRONMENTS AND EXPECTATIONS TO YOUR CHILD'S NEEDS

Given the power of the environment to affect your child's behavior, you may want to begin to think about how to create environments that are a good match for your child's differences and gifts. You don't have to lower your expectations for your child's level of achievement, but you should be sensitive to which directions are most likely to suit your child's natural abilities. An enormous amount of what looks like psychopathology can actually be the result of a terrible match between a person's natural gifts and her environment. For example, imagine how depressed and anxious a creative, artistic person would be while working as a computer programmer in a Fortune 500 company. Your child is stuck in a similar situation. Her gifts don't match the way in which most schools structure learning environments.

Although changing the school environment might not be feasible, you can keep your child's passions alive by building on your child's interests that won't be nurtured in the classroom. Very early, you can take seriously your child's interests in the natural world or other areas and begin providing guidance for how she might make a career out of these interests. As a general rule for activities and career directions, try to encourage your child in pursuits that build on existing strengths rather than trying to compensate for weaknesses.

It may seem way too early for you to think about career choices for your child, but your expectations deeply affect her perceptions of what is and what is not an acceptable direction to move in. Some children abandon interests at a very early age because parents convey that these interests aren't serious enough. But remember that any specialized area your child expresses interest in can be thought of as fuel for driving her interest in the academic arena. If she has an almost obsessive interest in dinosaurs, you can use that interest to get her engaged in reading books about dinosaurs or taking trips to natural history museums. If your child has an avid interest in sports, you can use that to develop her interest in math as she learns her favorite players' stats, records, and averages.

Sometimes parents make the mistake of suppressing interests that don't fit with their expectations for their child. A child who loves sports may later develop an interest in physical health in order to excel in sports, which may then transform into an interest in medicine. A child who loves to play with animals may develop knowledge and curiosity that leads her to a career as a veterinarian. Children who love listening to music may be motivated to learn to play and read it, which can facilitate the learning of math skills.

Similarly, your child's natural attunement to nature can be encouraged and can suggest directions for vocational interests later in life. Children with ADHD and a love of the outdoors can grow up to be conservationists, marine biologists, or county employees for managing and protecting water resources, for example. Although book learning is a struggle for individuals diagnosed with ADHD, if they achieve the discipline to make their way through higher education, they can make excellent doctors or veterinarians. While the rigors of a pre-med program and medical school are an obstacle, many ADHD students are capable of sticking through it. When they do, their sensuous consciousness serves them well as medical doctors, due to their intuitive connection with organic, living anatomy.

You do not need to provide career counseling for your young child, but you should not let your expectations deter your child from pursuing any interest that she is passionate about. Not only can her natural curiosity be channeled toward academic skills, but the interest itself can also become a content area that will serve her later in life.

On a much broader scale, your child's sensitivity may lead her to a satisfying career in conservation or preservation of the natural world. In that career, she may make a difference in the world, counteracting the current mind-set that devalues the environment and contributes to exploiting it for commercial ends.

SUMMARY

This chapter reviewed the way in which symptoms of ADHD can be seen as a form of ecological consciousness or engagement with the natural world. Rather than being a deficit or disorder, ADHD may represent a surplus of sensuous attunement with plants, trees, and animals.

CHAPTER 7

Interpersonal Intuition

Children with ADHD often cross interpersonal boundaries and display impulsive behavior that alienates their peers and teachers, leading to rejection and hurt feelings. One of the most painful aspects for parents of children diagnosed with ADHD to endure is to observe their child experiencing peer rejection. As challenging and painful as this experience can be, you can come to see your child's interpersonal style as a precocious but sometimes irreverent gift for understanding human interactions.

The following account illustrates how you, too, can transform your vision of the interpersonal style of ADHD.

A therapist in training, Amy Williams reported feeling anxious about her responsibilities as co-leader of a group therapy treatment for adolescent girls. Her anxiety as she assumed this new role was not surprising. As the group developed, her anxiety turned to dismay as she realized that one of the group members who had been diagnosed with ADHD was unmanageable. This member was loud and obnoxious and disrupted the group at every turn. Amy felt like she was losing control of the group and worked hard to keep it on track. After weeks of group therapy that seemed out of control because of the disruption caused by this one member, Amy mentally gave up. She walked into the next group meeting with the realization that she could not manage this group, and she would just have to stick it out. She accepted defeat and, in so doing, banished her anxiety. No longer was she intent on making the group work perfectly, nor was she doubting herself if she couldn't control its course.

Amy reported a remarkable transformation. The very day she conquered her anxiety, the group process transformed. The member who had been so disruptive was suddenly the model group client. The group therapy proceeded, and for the first time the process facilitated healing for all members.

In Amy's account of this remarkable transformation, the client with ADHD had been acting out Amy's anxiety about managing the group and her new role. And, as the client continued disrupting the group, Amy's anxiety escalated. A vicious circle was set in motion as the client's behavior grew worse and Amy became more anxious. As soon as Amy's anxiety dissipated, the vicious circle was stopped and the client's behavior was no longer disruptive or disturbed. Amy remarked that her first impressions of this client were that she was pretty superficial and incapable of connecting to others. Amy saw later that this client was in fact more connected to her than any other client was—she was so attuned to Amy's emotional state that she acted it out. Amy's transformation from seeing the client as superficial and obnoxious to seeing her as highly sensitive, attuned, and connected to her will serve as our template for understanding the interpersonal gifts of ADHD.

FREE-FLOATING AWARENESS

As shown in the story above, the intuitive ability of children diagnosed with ADHD bears a striking resemblance to the same gifts that therapists try to cultivate to understand their clients. Once recognized, the gift of intuition can be transformed into an ability to connect deeply with others.

Psychoanalysts utilize *free-floating awareness* as a way of picking up what clients may be feeling, and people with ADHD often have a similar form of awareness. It may allow the individual with ADHD to be strongly attuned to another person despite his inability to pay close attention to what the person is saying. This inability to listen carefully to others, a common symptom of ADHD, might be akin to what Freud called *evenly hovering attention,* which "simply consists in making no effort to concentrate the attention on anything in particular... [O]ne proceeds aimlessly, and allows oneself to be overtaken by any surprises, always presenting to them an open mind, free from any expectations" (1963, 118–20).

Freud thought that this form of attention was a talent necessary for listening with the *third ear,* or for developing interpersonal intuition. One of the gifts of children diagnosed with ADHD is this talent to discern what's not being said, or the ability to read the emotions of others.

One college student with ADHD reported that one of the reasons she had a hard time listening to others was that she so often recognized that what a person was saying contradicted what was really going on with him or her. She found herself paying close attention to a person's nonverbal cues, facial expressions, and gestures. Again, although it may have seemed like she was not paying attention at all, often she was very present and aware of the other person—just in ways that weren't typical. By this student's account, her inability to focus on the words being said allowed her to understand other people more deeply—because she wasn't guided simply by words. So, ADHD may be seen as an intuitive form of intelligence that picks up the present state of individuals, which they may not want to convey.

The problem for a child with ADHD is that he cannot stop his interpersonal intuition and sensitivity to others' emotions from flooding his experience. Because a child cannot process intense emotions, he will often resort to acting out the emotions of others in disruptive behavior. The exercises in this chapter will help your child channel his gift in productive ways.

Emotional Contagion

You can help your child understand his ability by describing it to him as "emotional contagion." Like a cold or a flu, other people's emotions can be caught, and your child is especially susceptible to catching them. This doesn't mean he's disabled or disordered—it simply allows him to understand others in a different and deeper way.

The steps to transforming this sensitivity into a gift are the following: (1) help your child become aware of the emotion he feels; (2) help him figure out whose emotions he is picking up; and (3) help him communicate his sensitivity to the person. There are also some strategies for helping your child protect himself from being too sensitive. The following exercises will help your child manage his emotional sensitivity to others.

EXERCISE: What Is This Feeling, and to Whom Does It Belong To?

Ask your child to remember an example of a behavior during which he felt out of control and which he couldn't explain at the time. As he tells you about the example, ask him who was most disrupted by the behavior or was the target of the behavior. Get as many concrete details as possible about the situation. It may be useful to start with an example that involves you, because then you can validate his feelings or explore them in greater depth.

When you have a very vivid picture in your mind of what happened, ask your child to take a few deep breaths and relax. Ask him to focus on what he was feeling at the time of the disruptive incident. You can help him by asking the following questions:

- Where do you feel it in your body?

- How big is the feeling?

- What color is the feeling?

- Is it hot or cold?

- Is it sharp or dull?

- Is it hard or soft?

- Does it make you more tired or give you more energy?

- What shape is it?

- Is it heavy or light?

- Is it strong or weak?

- Is it mad?

- Is it sad?

- Is it afraid?

- Is it excited?

- Is it happy?

- Is it upset?

- Is it disgusted?

- Is it surprised?

- What does it look like?

- Does it move?

- What name would you give it?

As you go through these questions, help your child get a strong impression of the emotion and help him define it or clarify the feeling.

Once your child has described the feeling, tell him that sometimes he may catch feelings from other people. He may start experiencing feelings that aren't really his. Then you might ask him to speculate about whose feeling it might have been. If the feeling involves a reaction to you, he might say, "I was just running around when you came to school to talk to the teacher. I didn't know why I couldn't stop, but I was afraid." You might want to explore whether *you* were afraid and he was sensitive to it. If you find that you were feeling fear in that situation, then you might say, "You are very sensitive to have picked up on that feeling, because I was nervous talking to your teacher. I was afraid he would think I was a bad mom, and I was afraid I would get mad at him for being impatient with you." In this way you may be able to validate his feelings, which mirrored your own. If the feelings aren't related to yours, you can still help him practice slowing down to think about the feeling, describe it in as much sensory detail as possible, and put a name on it.

Because children often act out feelings rather than feel them, helping your child slow down and feel, name, and describe what's going on inside of him will help manage his behavior. Once he is aware of his feelings, he won't act them out. Once he gains this awareness, he can talk about his feelings and can use his gift to increase intimacy with others. You can show your child how he can use his feeling to communicate a sense of connection with others. In the example above, you might suggest he ask you, "Are you afraid, Mommy?" As he begins translating his inner experience into a gift for connecting with others, people will respond differently to him.

The very same emotions that previously disrupted his behavior can now be channeled into forging connections with others.

After he practices this process with you, invite your child to practice applying it at school with his peers. You can role-play an interaction with a friend. For example, play a game of pretend. Ask your child to imagine that you are his cousin Kate. Describe a real-life example that ended in disruption. Remind your child of the time Kate's little brother started calling Kate names, for example. While Kate continued to play calmly, your child started throwing blocks at Kate's little brother. After going through the steps described above, encourage your child to practice saying to Kate something like the following: "I bet you're mad at your little brother. He's really acting like a pest." Then you can role-play Kate affirming your child, feeling even closer to your son, and continuing to play without disturbance.

EXERCISE: Force-Field Control

In this exercise you will help your child to protect himself from his emotional sensitivity. He will learn to use the feeling of being out of control as a signal that he is tuned in to someone else's emotional state.

1. Ask your child to identify how he knows when he is getting out of control. Ask him to identify the earliest warning signs he can think of. He may describe the experience of being overwhelmed, of feeling pushed, or of feeling like there is a motor in him making him do things. Whatever language he uses to describe the feeling, validate the feeling and tell him that this is an important warning sign that he needs to pay close attention to.

2. Ask him to spend a week paying attention to what he feels before, during, and after every episode of feeling out of control. During this week, you're not trying to change his behavior; you

are just trying to observe it. Every day after school, ask him how school went and if there was an incident where he felt out of control. Ask him to describe in as much detail, using the questions from the first exercise, what that out-of-control feeling was like. Any time you observe him losing control, ask him to stop and observe what that feels like.

3. Develop a detailed sensory description of what being out of control feels like. It may be something like "I feel like a rush of energy, and I can't stop myself. Sometimes I know I shouldn't do what I'm doing, but I feel like there is a jet engine making me move. I feel it as a stomachache, and usually it feels like a bright red color that's shaking." Have him elaborate on the description as much as possible.

4. Tell your child that he can think of this feeling as a warning signal. It means "Stop!" Ask your child to take one week to pay attention when he experiences this feeling. Whenever he gets the feeling during the week, he should practice stopping and taking a few breaths.

5. After having completed steps 1 through 4, teach your child to use an imaginary force field to provide a buffer between him and other people's emotions. Ask him to imagine that he has control over an invisible force field that can keep out impulses. Let him create this field in his imagination with as much embellishment as possible. For example, he may imagine a pink force field of energy that vibrates, and any impulses bounce off of it as soon as he senses them. Or he might imagine the field as a yellow bubble that surrounds him and protects him from impulses. Spend some time showing him how he can control this force field. He can make it go up, and he can make it go down. He can make it thicker or thinner. He can make it extend far from him or move closer to him. He can make it change color. He can make it stronger or weaker.

6. Tell your child that, for the next week, as soon as he feels his warning signal, he should practice using his force field. At the earliest sign that his warning signal is coming on, he can play this imaginary game.

7. When the week is over, ask your child to describe what happened when he used his force field. If the outcome was good, reinforce how much it helped and encourage him in using it. If the results were not as good as he'd hoped, help him problem solve and figure out how he could use it in a better way. Encourage him to keep practicing this imagination game.

FROM DEFIANT TO SELF-RELIANT

Children who have been diagnosed with ADHD are often perceived as interpersonally defiant or oppositional. It is this quality that most provokes teachers and sets up a negative interaction cycle. As you have discovered, the teacher's perception of and reaction to your child will have a powerful impact on his behavior, motivation, and success in school.

Because your child is so interpersonally sensitive, he will feel the teacher's judgment of him and act it out in class (or simply tune out and not try at all), setting up yet another vicious circle: Your child's teacher knows your child has been diagnosed with ADHD, so, at the first sign of disruption, she reacts very negatively. Your child picks up on the teacher's negative feelings and begins acting them out, causing even more disruption. Then the teacher punishes your child, embarrassing him. Now your child not only feels compelled to act out the teacher's increasingly negative feelings but also reacts strongly to being humiliated in class. Rather than being able to identify his feeling of being embarrassed by the teacher, your child is more likely to try to show the teacher he doesn't care by acting out even more. So the teacher's negative judgments and punitive behavior can create behavior that is, in fact, defiant—it is an attempt to defy the teacher's seeming rejection of your child.

So how does self-reliance fit into this process? Often, in this cycle, your child's initial behavior is a form of self-reliance that gets interpreted as defiance. The teacher's tendency to interpret self-reliance as defiance is what sets up the initial rejection, which leads to the cycle described above. For example, a common disruption involves a child getting out of his seat without asking permission. The reason he doesn't ask permission may be that he feels confident and does not want to bother the teacher. Imagine how different the situation would be if the teacher recognized the initial act of self-reliance rather than assuming that it represents defiance.

As mentioned earlier in the book, the teacher's interpretations of your child's behavior can have dramatic effects on his attitudes toward education and the course of his motivation and achievement. Research has found that teachers may be the force behind the dramatic increases in the diagnosis of ADHD. In one study, researchers who surveyed pediatricians, psychiatrists, and family physicians found that in 47 percent of cases of diagnosed ADHD, the teacher was the person who first suggested the diagnosis (Sax and Kautz 2003).

The implication of this finding is that teachers have a great deal of power in the diagnosis and course of ADHD. In light of this, as a parent who has a child diagnosed with ADHD, your efforts to work with the teacher are essential to your child's transformation. It also suggests that if your child's diagnosis was suggested by a teacher, you may want to consider the validity of the diagnosis. Although teachers don't make diagnoses, they usually are asked to fill out rating forms that psychologists and psychiatrists use in assessment. Often teachers are overworked, have too many children in their classes, and are working with too few resources. Their capacity to manage a class may be pushed to its limits due to increasing budget cuts in education, and therefore they may suggest that ADHD be treated with medications that make a child easier to control in the classroom. Teachers often have good intentions for your child, but they themselves have been schooled in the medical model of ADHD. They often believe that it is a medical disorder rather than a behavioral problem that can be caused and alleviated by changing thoughts, behavior, and environments.

The emphasis on control in the classroom serves the purpose of managing classes that are too large. But your child's best interests are served by teaching him to think for himself, to learn to trust his inner knowing—to be self-reliant. Success in the real world depends more on being able to think for oneself than on being able to sit still and memorize facts. On a much larger scale, the atrocities of Nazi Germany can, in part, be attributed to a nation that did not permit its citizens to think for themselves. On a smaller scale, you want your child to be able to think for himself as he becomes a teenager and is subject to strong peer pressures. For these reasons, as a parent you want to encourage your child's ability to think for himself. You will also want to advocate to teachers and school administrators that this capacity be appreciated.

There is a cultural element in your child's being labeled as oppositional or defiant. Ours is a culture that values teaching children conformity and compliance over self-reliance. This clashes with the tendencies of children with ADHD, who are often perceived as sensitive and charismatic (sometimes even the class clown). In tightly controlled classrooms, this charisma might be interpreted as defiance, and your child might be subjected to punishment and humiliation, which can then provoke actual defiance.

The increasing rates of diagnosis of ADHD may point to a failing in our educational system rather than a medical problem in your child. The terms *oppositional* and *defiant* are relational terms. One can only defy another person; it can only happen in a relationship, not in isolation. Therefore the labels may also be pointing to that which is being defied—in this case, very possibly the teacher, school, or overall educational system.

EXERCISE: Catch Your Child in Acts of Self-Reliance

In order for you to change your own interactions with your child and to become his advocate in school settings, you will need to practice changing your own interpretations of his behavior. Try the following exercise.

1. For one week, simply monitor your judgments of what you might think of as your child's oppositional behavior. Keep a journal of the behaviors that you felt were defiant, situations in which you wanted something and he refused or argued with you. Observe these situations, handle them as you usually do, and carefully note your reactions, your emotions, and the outcome of the situation. For example, you might write, "I told Steve that his friends had to go home because he had to clean up his bedroom before dinner. Steve got angry and said they were in the middle of a board game, and he wanted to finish. I felt impatient and tired, and I told Steve that he would not be able to have his friends over next week if he couldn't follow my directions. He started crying and got mad at me. His friends were obviously uncomfortable, and after they left Steve refused to clean his room and didn't talk at all during dinner."

2. For the next week, practice redefining your child's episodes of defiance as self-reliance in the moment. Try to see him as thinking for himself, and consider that he may be right. In many situations, this won't be appropriate: for example, if your child is cursing or hitting, you want to be sure to exert control in the situation. However, there is likely to be at least one situation in which your child may be right; in these situations, change your behavior to reflect your newfound appreciation of your child's self-reliance. As an example, if a situation like the one described above were to happen, you might note, "I told Steve that his friends had to go home because he had to clean up his bedroom

before dinner. Steve got angry and said they were in the middle of a board game, and he wanted to finish. As I watched him play, I saw that he and his friends were deeply engaged in an intense game of strategy. I realized they were at a critical point in their game and that it really wasn't a good time for them to stop. I commented to him and his friends about how challenging the game was, but I reminded Steve that dinner would be ready in twenty minutes. I told him that he could clean his bedroom after dinner, but that he would still have to finish the game in ten minutes so he could say good-bye to his friends and get cleaned up before dinner. Steve said that was okay, that in ten minutes they would reach a good stopping point."

3. Use your experience of reframing defiance as self-reliance to become an advocate for your child. Make an appointment to talk with his teachers and share your experience of how honoring your child's will in some circumstances has transformed your interactions from oppositional to respectful. You can also share how in the process you have seen new talents in him that you hadn't noticed before. Use some concrete examples to demonstrate for your child's teachers how they can practice reframing your child's oppositional behavior. Also share that you understand that the teacher needs to control and manage her classroom and that you understand that certain behaviors are far outside the limits. Let the teacher know that simply honoring your child's perspective on a few occasions each week can be enough to persuade your child that the teacher does see his perspective and is not simply out to get him.

This may seem like a lot of work to do. You may find yourself wishing that you didn't have to do so much for your child. It may seem like you're being asked to try to change the whole educational system. In some respects, that is exactly what you are doing. Each parent who advocates for change may begin to envision what we want for our children's education overall. There are effective models for teaching children besides the ones that place the highest emphasis on conformity, compliance, and control. Parents can play a role in shaping the demand for a different vision. In helping your child to transform his problems into strengths, you may even find yourself on the path of becoming a social activist.

SUPPORT YOUR CHILD'S SUCCESS

As you introduce some of these new exercises and your child begins to identify his own emotions and see them as sensitivity to others, you'll be able to notice your child engaging in interpersonal interactions with you and others in a new way. Pay special attention to what your child is doing right. This will not only serve to reinforce or reward your child for transforming his behavior but also help you problem solve around other interpersonal difficulties.

Sometimes problems are simply the result of unfortunate learned behaviors. For example, if your child blurts out inappropriate comments in social settings, it may be because he finds the eye-popping, jaw-dropping reactions he gets from adults to be stimulating. Your child may be interpreting these visual cues as positive reinforcement. Remember that a major interpersonal gift of ADHD is that these children are tuned in to people's emotional reactions and attend more to nonverbal cues than to what adults actually say.

Additionally, sometimes bad behavior can be easily managed by working on solving problems in the conditions preceding such behavior. For example, Sharon found that her daughter, Frances, would bully her younger brother in the morning when they were getting ready for school. When Sharon began looking for times when this behavior did not occur or when Frances was helpful toward her younger brother, she noticed one morning (Frances's birthday) when things ran very smoothly—Frances didn't bully her brother, and the family was able to get out of the house without any major meltdowns. As Sharon drove her daughter to school, she expressed her appreciation and asked her what was different about this morning. Frances said that because it was her birthday they had spent the night before picking out her outfit and braiding her hair. When she woke up that morning, all she had to do was put on the outfit she had already picked out and eat breakfast. Frances explained that since she was all ready to go in the morning, she didn't mind her little brother following her around, because she didn't have to worry about being late.

By catching her daughter doing something right and asking "What went right?" Sharon was able to change a longstanding interpersonal problem between her two children. Sharon had always thought that the morning tantrums and meltdowns were because her daughter had ADHD. When Sharon went out of her way to catch her daughter doing something right, she uncovered the real cause of the morning meltdowns—her daughter had a lot on her mind and a lot to do, and she rightly perceived her little brother as getting in her way in the morning rush.

Paying attention when your child does something right leads to positive reinforcement, which is likely to increase the good behavior. In addition, by asking "What went right?" you can solve specific problems and eliminate bad behavior. In Sharon's case, she changed the family routine so that either she or her husband spent some time in the evening helping their daughter prepare for school the next day. They picked out clothes, they planned hairstyles, they packed backpacks, and they even planned breakfast. Frances could then get up in the morning without pressure and not feel bothered by her little brother. Sharon found that making this simple change dramatically transformed mornings in their home.

By changing this one behavior, Sharon also saw how each behavior had been a part of a powerful chain reaction that escalated the tension in the home. When Frances was stressed out and trying to get ready, she would tease her little brother. Her little brother would cry, and Sharon would have to separate them and comfort her son. As Sharon quelled these fights, she knew she herself was becoming late and worried that she would not get to work on time.

As she became more worried about work, she got mad at Frances for seeming to cause all these problems and for putting this additional stress on the family. As Sharon got increasingly mad, Frances's bad behavior escalated because she was so sensitive to her mother's anger. Frances usually acted out her mother's anger by hitting her brother. Once she had hit her brother, a family meltdown was well on its way to happening.

Before, it seemed like Frances was the sole cause of all the morning tension; now, on reflection, Sharon could see that each family member's reactions led to a cycle that escalated the tension. By paying attention when things went well, Sharon was able to turn this cycle around and stop blaming Frances, which changed the family dynamic. Sharon's story illustrates not only the power of actively searching for your child doing something right but also the power of the ADHD label on your perception of him.

When you interpret your child's behavior as the cause of, rather than a reflection of, family tensions, your sensitive child easily senses the blame he's subject to and internalizes an image of himself as bad. The more the diagnosis causes you to blame him for family tensions, even if you don't express this blame verbally, the more he will feel the blame and internalize it. And the more he blames himself, the more he tends to think of himself as bad and unable to control his behavior. The more he thinks of himself this way, the more his behavior will reflect this internal image.

EXERCISE: What Went Right?

This exercise will help you to change the dynamic of blame and bad behavior in your family.

1. Catch your child doing something right. Watch for an instance in which your child does not engage in a habitual bad behavior or when he has a positive interaction.

2. Ask yourself and your child, "What went right? What was different? What preceded the good behavior? What followed the good behavior? Why were things different?" Get as many details as possible.

3. Ask yourself, "In what ways is this bad behavior a reflection of family tensions rather than the cause of family tensions?"

4. Make changes in family routines as appropriate. If this exercise reveals more deep-seated problems, seek counseling or outside help. For example, a child with ADHD may act out negative feelings stemming from marital conflict between the parents or unresolved depression and grief experienced by one or both parents. You or your partner, or both of you as a couple, might need to work with a therapist in order to resolve an underlying conflict or tension that your child is reflecting back to you.

SUMMARY

In this chapter, we have reviewed how symptoms of ADHD can be seen as an interpersonal gift. Children diagnosed with ADHD are very sensitive to the emotions of the people around them. They are prone to emotional contagion, or reflecting and acting out unexpressed emotions of people they feel connected with. This ability can lead to interpersonal disturbances, but it can also be channeled to reveal and enhance your child's emotional sensitivity and deep connection with others.

CHAPTER 8

Your Exuberant Child: Reframing Hyperactivity

If you're like most adults in our culture, you suffer from a sort of hypoactivity disorder—not having enough energy. Rates of depression, chronic fatigue syndrome, and sleep deprivation are skyrocketing in our culture. In short, we are tired. Don't you wish you had a lot more energy? Wouldn't that be a gift?

If your child has a lot of energy, then she is already blessed with that gift. But because she may have what seems like an excess of energy, she may have received the "hyperactive" label. However, what doctors and teachers call hyperactivity can also be called exuberance. Exuberance is characterized by high energy and an intense interest in and curiosity about the world. Exuberant children are often playful, intense, and fun to be around. So why does a trait that seems so obviously positive get turned into a disorder? As a parent of a child with this diagnosis, you are well aware that your child's excess of energy demands a lot of energy from you and her teachers. While the focus of this chapter will be how to reframe this surplus of energy as a gift, it is worth considering, in passing, whether the increasing rate of ADHD diagnoses in children parallels the increasing rate of depression in the adult population. Both of these diagnoses are subjective, so if teachers and parents are reporting increasingly low levels of energy, then by comparison our children may look like they have abnormally high levels of energy.

Even so, your child with ADHD likely shows higher levels of energy and activity than other children her age. This chapter will help you and your child increase your family's appreciation for this high level of energy. You will learn two complementary strategies for helping you to manage your child. The first strategy will involve techniques to help your child contain her high level of energy, so she can avoid immediately and impetuously acting out her impulses. The second strategy involves finding ways to channel your child's energy that reveal it as a resource rather than a difficulty.

APPRECIATING AND MANAGING YOUR CHILD'S HIGH ENERGY

One of the reasons high energy becomes a problem in children is that the energy seems to have a mind of its own. It exists at the service of an unfolding urge or impulse felt by the child and is not directed toward productive ends. The essential problem is that the energy is unfocused.

However, you and your child can learn to view her surplus of energy as a valuable resource. You can help your child learn to take charge of this energy, rather than being driven by it.

EXERCISE: Taking Over the Steering Wheel

Many children with the diagnosis of ADHD describe feeling like they have an internal motor that makes them go all the time. This exercise has two elements. In the first part, your child will practice monitoring her internal "motor" activity. By becoming aware of her motor, she will be less likely to be driven by it, and she will gain skills to help her tolerate the driven feeling. In the second part, your child will make fun cards with positive reminders telling her that she can control herself and take charge of the energy.

1. To begin, talk to your child about how her excess energy can be thought of as a powerful motor that drives her. Ask her to draw a picture of the motor. Encourage her to talk about what the motor feels like and how fast it makes her go. Ask her to pay attention to the motor while she's at school and just notice when it speeds up or slows down during the day.

2. While driving her home from school, or once she gets home, check in with your child and ask her what she noticed about the motor. Listen carefully as she tells you about her experience. Here are some questions you might ask her:

    *   Where in your body do you feel the motor?

    *   How big is the motor?

    *   How fast is it?

    *   What color is it?

    *   When does the motor speed up?

    *   What happens before it speeds up?

    *   What happens after it speeds up?

    *   When does it slow down?

- What happens right before it slows down?

- What happens right after it slows down?

Use some of your child's responses to suggest strategies for giving her control of the motor. For example, if your child says she notices the motor speed up when she sits next to her friend Tommy during reading group, you can suggest that she try not sitting next to Tommy during reading group. If she says she noticed her motor slow down when she was trying to fix one of the toys at school, suggest to her that, when she finds her motor revving up, she can find something to fix or tinker with. You can also suggest to her teacher that your child be given certain responsibilities that involve tinkering, such as setting up audiovisual equipment, as a strategy for calming her down. You can also suggest to the teacher that he value and praise her abilities. Similarly, at home you may want to offer a great deal of validation and approval of her work with mechanical objects. In this way, she can receive approval and increase her self-worth by doing activities that are intrinsically rewarding to her.

Make a fun game out of creating cards that remind your child that she can control the motor. You will need 3 by 5 or 4 by 6 index cards. Tell your child that she can notice when the motor revs up and take charge by imagining that she is driving a car, with her hands on the steering wheel and her feet on the brakes. She can cut out and paste pictures of cars or boats, or draw her own, on one side of the cards. On the other side, you can write out reminders for your child, such as the following:

- I can slow down the motor.

- I can steer the car.

- If I take a few deep breaths, I can put on the brakes.

- If I take time to feel the motor, I can take charge.

- I'm in charge.

- I can use this motor to help me pay attention.

- I can use this motor to help the teacher.

- I can use this motor to help other students.

- I can use this motor to do my homework.

- I can use this motor to clean my room.

- I know how to slow down the motor.

- I can put my hands on the steering wheel.

- I can sit still even if the motor is going fast.

- I can stay quiet just by noticing the motor.

Have your child take these cards to school and keep them at her desk. You can also keep a second set around the house, to use as reminders of how to channel energy in positive ways. The more your child is involved in having fun in creating the cards, the more she'll be interested in looking at them and using them in school and other settings. After a day or two, ask your daughter to tell you about how and when she has used the cards in school. Listen carefully and offer generous praise for using the cards and taking control of her behavior, and help her problem solve if trouble arises. For example, if other kids make fun of her cards, suggest ways she can handle the situation by standing up for herself or help her figure out how to use the cards in a way that won't draw the attention of other students. You might also want to let the teacher know that your child will be using the cards.

The above exercise combines some of the most fundamental cognitive behavioral strategies for transforming behavior. First, you guide your child in monitoring her behavior, because awareness generally precedes any change. By simply noticing the revved-up, driven feeling, your child will be taking a significant step toward gaining control. The more she is aware of the driven feeling, the less she will impulsively act out. Next, by identifying antecedents and consequences of behavior, you and she work to shape her behavior.

In addition to the behavior strategies in the above exercise, you will want to make changes in your child's environment so that those situations that precede the motor slowing down occur more frequently. Similarly, you will want to change her environment to reduce or eliminate situations that cause her motor to speed up. Also, when your child notices the positive consequences of the motor slowing down, she will begin to notice the subsequent rewards and may become more aware of the negative results when the motor speeds up. For example, your child will likely report that one consequence of the motor speeding up is out-of-control behavior that gets negative responses from teachers and other students. By simply observing how these consequences follow from changes in the speed of her internal motor, she will change her behavior to increase the frequency of positive responses.

In your journal, record all the information you get from your child about what comes before, after, and during the changes in motor speed. After a few weeks of taking notes, summarize your findings under the following titles:

- Behaviors That Slow the Motor Down

- Behaviors That Speed the Motor Up

- Consequences of Speeding the Motor Up

- Consequences of Slowing the Motor Down

Once you have compiled a fairly long list of behaviors under each title, you can shape your child's environment to help her manage her behavior according to the information you have collected. Your goal is to (1) increase the activities or events that slow the motor down and (2) decrease or eliminate activities that speed the motor up.

Tell your child's teachers about the information you've gathered to help her manage her behavior while at school. Share the information with your child as well, to help her keep in mind the importance of paying attention to her inner motor. By reminding her of the negative consequences of a revved-up motor and the positive consequences of a slowed-down motor, you will help her increase her motivation to exercise control over her motor.

Revving Down the Motor

The preceding exercise provides powerful suggestions to your child that she is in charge. These suggestions and positive expectations can themselves effect changes in your child's behavior. They are helpful in counteracting the message she may get from teachers and doctors that ADHD is impossible to control without medication. In addition to increasing her perception that she can begin to control her behavior, you can give her specific techniques for slowing down the motor.

Children live in the worlds of their imagination, and research shows that imagination can have powerful effects on feelings, thoughts, and even physical health problems (VanKuiken 2004). Your child's imagination can become a powerful resource for containing and channeling her high levels of energy. Following are a few pretend games your child can try. Some of them she'll like; others she won't. Try a few and repeat only the ones that are most fun for your child. If it feels like a chore, your child won't be motivated to use it. If none of the games clicks with your child, try to make up your own images or pretend games that serve the same function.

EXERCISE: The Speedometer

Tell your child you are going to play a pretend game in which she'll use her powers of imagination. Ask her to sit down and take a few deep breaths. Then tell her to imagine a control room, perhaps an airplane cockpit, that contains a lot of dials and control valves. Invite her to playfully explore this control room. Ask her to find a gauge that tells her how fast her motor is revving. Ask her to imagine that the gauge goes from 0 to 100 miles per hour, then ask her to tell you what the speed is now. Tell your child that, just as you can adjust a thermostat to change the temperature in a room, she can change the speed of her motor by adjusting a powerful control valve. Tell her to imagine finding the control valve that determines the speed of the motor. When she finds it, ask her to slow down the motor speed. If it was at 50 miles per hour, tell her to move it to 20 miles per hour. Ask her how this level of energy feels. Then have her experiment until she finds a specific speed that feels comfortable—a speed at which she has enough energy to focus and pay attention but not so much that she still feels driven or can't sit still.

Practice this repeatedly, and remind your child that she can use the control valve to change the speed of her motor. Remind her of her target speed, and tell her that she should use the control valve to get to that speed whenever she feels she has too little or too much energy.

Spend some time playing with your child to make the control valve and gauge concept more concrete. She can draw the room or cockpit where the gauge and control valve are located, depicting both of these items in detail. If you can find any toys that look similar to the valve, have her physically act out these control strategies.

In addition, ask her to draw a gauge on a blank index card with the needle pointed at the most comfortable speed for her internal motor. She can take this card to school to keep at her desk as a reminder that she can control her energy level. You can also have her carry a card that has a picture or drawing of her control valve. On the other side of the card you can write, "I'm in charge!"

EXERCISE: Gamma Ray Bursts

Children are often full of wonder about the universe, planets, and deep space. You can tap into this interest to help inspire your child to work on focusing her intense energy. A particularly inspiring example is gamma ray bursts, which are the brightest explosions since the big bang (Nadis 2004). Gamma ray bursts have the highest energy blasts yet found by astronomers, but what makes them particularly special is that the energy is not sprayed in all directions but is focused into narrow beams or jets. They are powerful, energetic bursts caused by the explosion of a star, and the energy is channeled like a laser beam.

Tell your child about this fascinating scientific discovery and let her know that she can be like a gamma ray burst by focusing her powerful energy like a laser beam. Tell her to imagine focusing her energy on whatever task is at hand. For example, if she has worksheets to do for homework and has too much energy to sit still, remind her of the gamma ray burst. Tell her that right now her energy is like an explosion, with all the energy going off in every direction but not able to accomplish anything. Tell her that she can focus her energy like the gamma ray burst and use it to get her homework done. You can have her draw pictures of what a gamma ray burst would look like and put it on an index card to take to school with her. On the other side of the card you can write, "I can focus my energy like a gamma ray burst." You might also want to track down gamma ray burst photos from the January 2004 issue of *Astronomy*, the *National Geographic* website, or other astronomy sites on the Internet. These photos can provide powerful mental images for your child, reminding her that she can control and focus her energy.

If you try these two games and your child's interest is not piqued, work with her to develop an image or game that is fun for her. If she has a passionate interest in a sport, video game, or movie character, use her specialized interest to develop a game or visual image that will help her channel and transform her high levels of energy.

REDIRECTING THIS POWERFUL RESOURCE

Even though your child's high level of energy can seem like a tremendous drain on your own energy, you can begin to think of it as a resource. It's important to remember that, though you can expect improvements in your child's control of her energy, you cannot expect to entirely quell your child's high energy level and sense of being driven. If you keep this in mind, you will be more open to parenting strategies that will lead to improvements in your relationship with your child.

Staying Positive

Parents of children diagnosed with ADHD often wind up punishing their child for bad behavior or academic failure by increasing the level of demands for quiet time or academic study. Unfortunately, this tactic is not effective, because your child's high energy is not willful—it is a reservoir that she needs to learn specific skills to manage. By punishing your child, you communicate that she is wrong rather than simply different.

Another problem with punishing children diagnosed with ADHD is that most forms of punishment, while unpleasant for all children, are excruciating for children with ADHD. For example, sending a child to her room, prescribing quiet time, and taking away a favorite activity are punishments that are more difficult for a child with ADHD to endure successfully. For this reason, your child will likely appear to defy your demands for quiet time. This looks like defiance, which seems to warrant even more punishment, thus setting up yet another vicious circle.

As a general rule, it is better to use positive reinforcement strategies for any child, but particularly for a child diagnosed with ADHD. One reason for this is that your child likely experiences rejection and failure at school and desperately needs a safe place at home where she can feel accepted for who she is. To the extent that you can eliminate punishment from your parenting repertoire, you will improve your relationship with your child and serve her more effectively.

Positive reinforcement means actively looking for positive behaviors or the absence of negative behaviors and offering praise and rewards for this. In short, you want to catch your child doing something right. This dramatic shift in parenting a difficult child can be hard, since you may have built up a lot of frustration and want to do what works most quickly. But it's important to remember the long-term toll that punishment takes on your child's self-esteem and self-worth. Though it may feel like a quick fix, punishment will reduce self-esteem, leading to long-term aggravation of existing behavior problems. It requires some thought and energy on your part to determine how you will offer praise or rewards. But the long-term payoffs are often substantial. Positive reinforcement will improve your relationship with your child because she won't feel bad about herself or be angry with you for taking something she likes away from her. The stronger your relationship with your child, the more "capital" you have for negotiating behavior change rather than enforcing it. Let's now look at ways for you to build your capital with your child.

The Power of Responsibility

One of the more effective strategies for managing your child's behavior might be called "preventative behavioral management." Knowing what your child is good at and what she continually struggles with, you can begin to channel her energy in productive ways that will prevent behavioral problems from occurring. For example, your child has a basic need to be active and engaged in some form of hands-on project, even more so than other children. You can use this to your advantage. Instead of punishing your child after a behavioral problem has occurred, you can prevent bad behavior by practicing a simple strategy: giving your child responsibility for specific projects that are of interest to her and are helpful to you.

The first transformative principle of this strategy is that, by giving your child responsibility, you are conveying your trust and confidence in her. Rather than making her do household chores as a punishment for bad behavior, you can convey that you are entrusting her with this project, which would be of great benefit to the family. You are framing your request as a reward. For example, if you catch your child engaging in good behavior, you can say that since she is showing so much improvement, you would like to give her the responsibility of a special project.

It is important to be thoughtful about the project you assign, and match the project to something that your child might enjoy. For example, you could give her something broken that could be fixed or at least tinkered with, if she likes that kind of task, or you could ask her to fold laundry or empty the garbage. As described in a previous chapter, children with ADHD tend to find it calming to spend time in nature, so you might ask your child to do some landscaping or pull weeds, which would be a good use of her high energy and give her some time outside. By using this strategy, you can begin to think of your child's high energy as a resource rather than a defect.

Many people love to fix broken objects, get their hands dirty, and manually labor to clean things up or improve the environment. These tasks can be even more enjoyable for children with ADHD, who benefit greatly from sensuous engagement with the world. Children with ADHD often like to see something get solved or accomplished. In part, this relates to their frustration with schoolwork: it is abstract and seems unrelated to everyday life. As a parent you can take advantage of this frustration by directing your child's energy and intelligence toward solving real-life problems and improving the environment, even the home environment.

It is also important that you convey respect for these tasks. Our culture undervalues this sort of work and considers it to be menial labor, instead placing an over-emphasis on book learning and school achievement. So parents often use these sorts of tasks as punishment for bad behavior because they don't value this physical work. But you can do the opposite and view it as useful and even therapeutic for your child.

The second transformative principle of this strategy is that it channels your child's energy, keeping her entertained and occupied in what will seem to her a meaningful activity. This will prevent her from getting in more trouble and will also be calming in itself, due to the sensory, concrete nature of the task. This calming effect will give your child more ability to focus on schoolwork or other tasks requiring focused, abstract attention.

Following are two scenarios that contrast the use of punishment with the use of positive reinforcement and giving your child responsibility for household projects.

SCENARIO 1: PUNISHMENT

You are mother to two young girls. After school one balmy day, your daughter Robin tells you that she wants to go play baseball with some friends. You tell her no, saying that she doesn't have time, because you will all be taking her sister to an appointment. Robin starts crying and gets angry that she can't go play. Her emotional display quickly turns into a full-blown tantrum with loud yelling. You raise your voice and tell Robin to control herself, but she doesn't. You tell her she has to calm down now or she will not get to watch TV this evening. She seems to lose control even more and cries even more loudly. Raising your voice, you tell her that she needs to get herself ready to leave the house and to get in the car. After many threats, she pulls herself together, still crying and sulking, and drags herself to the car. During the appointment, Robin runs around the waiting room and loudly asks you if she gets to watch TV tonight. You say you will talk about it at home, and she complains louder and louder.

That night, you tell her that instead of watching TV with the family she has to go to her room. While in her room she whines loudly that it's not fair, cries, and creates messes by throwing her toys around aggressively. Her father asks her to be quiet and reminds her that this is the consequence of her temper tantrum. Robin continues to complain loudly that it's not fair. Her father tells her that if she doesn't stop whining, she won't be able to watch TV the next night. Robin starts crying again and yelling that no one cares about her. After her father leaves, Robin starts thinking that something must be really wrong with her because she cannot control her behavior. She feels very alone because she thinks her parents are mad at her, and when they're angry she doesn't feel like she can talk to them.

SCENARIO 2: RESPONSIBILITY AND POSITIVE REINFORCEMENT

Robin tells you that she wants to go play baseball with some friends. You tell her no, saying that she doesn't have time, because you will all be taking her sister to an appointment. Robin starts crying and gets angry that she can't go play. Her emotional display quickly turns into a full-blown tantrum with loud yelling. You walk away without giving her any attention while she has the tantrum. After a few minutes of crying and yelling, Robin realizes that no one is paying any attention to her. She sees that you are rushing around looking for something. She says, "What are you looking for, Mommy?" You tell her you cannot find the keys. She runs around the house looking for the keys and finds them for you. When she gives you the keys, you say to her, "Thank you so much, Robin. Whew! You're a lifesaver. You have been so helpful. You're doing such a great job helping me out and helping all of us get your sister to her appointment on time." In the car on the way to the appointment, you say to Robin, "Since I can see you're trying so hard to help out the family, I want to give you responsibility for a project. I want you and your dad to work together to make something to hold all the family keys so we won't lose them so easily." Robin gets really excited about the idea and starts telling you all the ideas she has for how to make a key holder to hang in the front hallway. While you're in the waiting room at her sister's appointment, Robin continues to talk about her ideas for the key holder.

That night, when her father comes home, Robin excitedly tells him about the key holder that Mom said she could help him make.

She tells her dad about all of her different ideas. Dad tells her that if she does some of her worksheets for school after dinner, they can run to the hardware store to get some of the material for the key holder. Robin jumps up and down because she is so excited to go to the hardware store. She says she will do her worksheets so she can go to the store to pick out the stuff.

HOW THE STRATEGIES COMPARE

As you can see, the difference between punishment and positive reinforcement has dramatic consequences for your child's behavior and your relationship with her. In the second scenario, when you chose to ignore the temper tantrum, you were taking away one reinforcer for such behavior—the attention that Robin gets by engaging in the behavior. It may be that by throwing a temper tantrum your child successfully takes your attention away from something else and puts it back on herself. Although your attention in such cases is negative, it may be experienced as rewarding for a child. In fact, children can often stop a temper tantrum quickly if it doesn't receive any attention, positive or negative. Additionally, over time temper tantrums will be less likely to occur if they are not given attention. Just ensure that your child is safe and make sure that she doesn't engage in any behaviors that could hurt herself or others.

More important than not reinforcing bad behavior is to offer positive reinforcements for good behavior. In the above scenario, when you offered Robin a project to work on, she was able to channel her high energy into the new project. Rather than tearing up the doctor's waiting room, she could excitedly plan for this new project. In this case, the child got a boost to her self-esteem and felt the need to live up to the responsibility she was given. In addition, the project gave her an avenue for connecting with her father.

Positive reinforcement is effective because not only will it increase the good behavior, it will increase your child's self-worth and her sense of connection to you. If your child feels that you value her, she will be more likely to feel she can share her thoughts and feelings with you. The more she can share with you, the stronger your relationship will be. The strength of your relationship with your child is the single most powerful factor in preventing bad behavior.

SELF-CARE FOR THE PARENT

Parents of ADHD children are often in desperate need of finding ways to increase their own energy level in order to work effectively with their high-energy children. The quickest way to raise your energy level is to take your own needs and passions seriously. Many parents feel guilty if they spend time, money, and resources to honor their own needs. However, the parent's well-being has a direct impact on the child's. To put it simply, if your energy is high, then you will be more capable of connecting with your high-energy child.

Get out a piece of paper and a pencil, and write at the top "I would be delighted to..." Then write down the first ten things that come to mind. Choose at least two to put into action this week. By feeding your own passions and needs, you will be reenergized. You will also serve as a better model for your child as you teach her how to care for herself. Taking your passions seriously may be as simple as signing up for a tap-dance class, or as complex as restructuring your entire family's schedule in order to simplify your home life. Begin taking a small first step in the direction of meeting your own needs.

SUMMARY

Your child's energy can make her exuberant, charismatic, and fun to be around, but it can also make her a challenging force for parents and teachers. This chapter reviewed the way in which symptoms of hyperactivity can be seen as a valuable resource. If your child can learn to focus her high levels of energy, she can use what is seen as a negative symptom to fuel productive accomplishment. If you follow the techniques in this chapter, this high energy level can be transformed so that she can use it to achieve her goals.

CHAPTER 9

Your Emotionally Expressive Child

One of the symptoms parents of children with ADHD struggle with most is their child's emotional outbursts. Children with ADHD have little emotional control. When they're sad, they are given to fits of crying; when they're angry, they are given to tantrums; and when they are excited, they're prone to act like a Tasmanian devil, whirling around and leaving big messes as they go. Not only do they tend toward big displays of emotion, but they also seem to be subject to a more frequent loss of emotional control than other children, leaving parents to cringe inside and dread social situations where they expect their child to throw a temper tantrum.

However, these very same symptoms that parents may have come to dread represent a remarkable gift: emotional sensitivity and intensity. Your child may be prone to more frequent emotional reactions because he is so responsive and sensitive to life, to other people, and to his connection with others. Children with ADHD go through each day living in a world that has the volume turned up much higher than it is for others. This quality of emotional sensitivity may be seen as the fundamental distinctive feature of ADHD and can be seen as helping to drive the other gifts of ADHD.

The gift of emotional sensitivity is directly related to the gift of interpersonal intuition. Our interpersonal relationships and sense of connection to others depend on emotional sensitivity. We connect with others by understanding how they feel. Remember how President Bill Clinton moved our nation by saying "I feel your pain"? Children with ADHD have this same capacity. The more emotionally sensitive a child is, the more he can empathize with others because he has felt those same emotions. Your child has this gift of sensitivity in abundance.

The gift of emotional sensitivity is also directly related to the gift of creativity. Because the world affects your child more deeply, his capacity to represent the world in artistic ways is increased. He can see things others cannot see and feel things that others just barely notice. His perception of the world strikes us as creative because it is different.

Further, the gift of intense emotional experience fuels your child's deep connection to the natural and organic world. Whereas for many adults the natural world is merely part of the background, the child diagnosed with ADHD is intensely sensitive to the organic, growing, alive, nurturing qualities of the natural world. Your child's ecological intelligence is related to a sensitivity to and concern for his environment. Because the volume is turned up on the world, your child can feel attuned to plants, animals, trees, and other aspects of the natural landscape. As noted in chapter 6, this capacity is much needed in the world today in order to promote conservation and preservation of natural resources.

In addition, emotional expressivity is also directly related to your child's surplus of energy. His intense emotions are like a high-powered fuel compelling him to give behavioral expression to his intense experiences. In fact, hyperactivity is a behavioral strategy that allows your child to discharge high levels of emotional experiences. It's hard to sit still and focus attention with such powerful emotions coursing through one's body and mind.

EMOTIONAL SENSITIVITY AND EMOTIONAL EXPRESSION

Transforming emotional intensity from a symptom into a gift involves helping your child to separate emotional sensitivity from emotional expression.

There is an automatic quality to your child's behavior: impulses are immediately followed by behavior. And this is true in all children, because the part of the brain that controls emotional expression is still developing—so the capacity to control emotions is a skill all children must learn. A child diagnosed with ADHD shares this lack of control, but it's paired with an emotional experience of a much greater magnitude than in other children. The intense emotion felt by a child with ADHD typically does not enter his awareness—it just gets acted out impulsively and discharged.

This chapter will offer an exercise for reining in emotional sensitivity, but our emphasis will be on breaking the pattern of intense emotion that is automatically followed by an intense emotional outburst. Your child will learn how to maintain his sensitivity without disrupting the environment with intense displays of emotion.

EXERCISE: Helping Your Child Ask for Help

In this exercise, the goal is simply to increase your child's awareness of the difficulty of managing his emotions. By increasing his awareness of his struggle, he can be guided to ask for help. By asking for help, your child will increase his chances of channeling his intense emotions in socially appropriate ways. Because every social situation is singular, you cannot give your child a simple formula to help him develop social skills.

The most important aspect of the following exercise is that it reminds your child to put one step—a request for help—between emotional expression and emotional outburst. By directing your child to ask for help, you're offering him a strategy for breaking the automatic pattern in a way that seems reasonable to your child. By giving him help, you are acknowledging that the intensity of his emotions may prevent him from rationally deciding how to effectively channel his sensitivity. Most important, you are giving him a wedge to insert between a strong emotion and a socially inappropriate behavior. Just that one step between the emotion and action may be all that it takes to break the pattern of disruptive behavior.

Start by talking with your child about his emotional intensity and reframing it for him as a gift. Give many examples, like the following, of how emotional sensitivity is a much-needed trait in the world.

- Emotional sensitivity helps us to connect with others by showing them we know what they are feeling.

- It helps us see parts of the world that need to be fixed.

- It helps us see people who need our attention.

- It helps us know our own selves.

- It can lead to creativity.

- It helps you to care for other people.

Talk to your child about how there is a difference between our strong feelings and our behavior. Let him know that you can feel something strongly and not act it out in ways that disrupt others. Tell him that because he is so gifted with emotional sensitivity, he may need to ask for help from adults in order to find positive ways of expressing his emotions. Tell your child that, whenever he feels a strong emotion that begins to feel uncontrollable, he should ask a trusted adult (such as his teacher at school, you, or his other parent) to help him with it.

For one week, practice this with your child at home. Whenever you notice him getting highly emotional, remind him to ask for help. If you catch him after his behavior has gotten out of control, avoid acting angry at him; instead, remind him that next time, he can ask for help before he loses control. Reassure him that he does not have to figure out how to control himself. All that he has to do is ask for assistance.

After practicing for a week, ask your child to practice this at school. You will want to let his teachers know what you're working on. You may want to share with the teachers some specific strategies you have discovered in your weeklong trial period. Once he has had a chance to practice this strategy at school, look for a time when your child is in a positive and calm frame of mind, and ask him the questions that follow. Write his responses in a journal.

- What can you do to help yourself when your emotions start to feel too big for you?

- What can we (your parents) do to help you when your emotions start to feel too big?

- What can your teachers do to help you when your emotions start to feel too big?

- What can your brother and sister do to help you when your emotions start to feel too big?

- What can your friends and classmates do to help you when your emotions start to feel too big?

As you go about your activities, begin to try some of the suggestions your child comes up with. For one week, when he asks for your help, guide him to ask for the aid that he identified as helpful. For example, your child might tell you that when he gets mad at his little brother and asks for help, he wants you to not only separate him and his brother physically but also show that you understand why he is mad. So, the next time your child gets mad and asks for help, do what he has asked: separate him and his brother and reassure him that you can see why he got frustrated at his brother.

In trying this exercise, you can expect to transform your child's behavior just by guiding him to insert one action—asking for help—between his intense emotion and his impulsive action. By doing this, you are not repressing your child's sensitivity but helping him to gain social skills in one social situation after another. As he learns to get help, he will gradually gain the skills and strategies he needs to stay connected to his own gifted emotional life without disrupting the environment.

Often you will find that the more you validate the intense emotion your child feels, the more he'll be able to gain control. Any time you can immediately validate the feeling while channeling its expression, you can defuse a potential outburst. It is paradoxical that the more you negate, criticize, or deny your child's feeling, the more it will grow out of control; similarly, the more you validate it, the smaller it will get. You'll be amazed at the power of this one technique.

Here's another example of how this strategy plays out. Imagine that your child is jealous because you are spending a lot of time nursing his baby brother. You will help him to gain control by deeply affirming his feelings: "Of course you want some of the attention that your little brother gets now. It's okay if sometimes you feel mad at him when Mommy's nursing him. But remember to ask me for help when you're mad rather than jumping up on Mommy when she nurses your little brother." In this way, you do not make him feel like he is a bad person for having his feelings. The worse he feels about himself, the more his behavior is likely to be disruptive. The more he sees his feelings as acceptable, the more he will be motivated to work with you to help manage them. Figure that you will have to remind your child frequently to ask for help in the early stages of using this strategy.

In addition, this simple technique of labeling your child's emotions has been found to have long-lasting positive impacts. One recent study found that children with mothers who talk to them about emotional states have significantly better social skills than children with mothers who don't talk about emotional states (Yuill et al. 2007; also Ruffman, Slade, and Crowe 2002). So, by frequently labeling your child's emotions and talking about other people's emotions, you are preparing your child for both emotional intelligence and high-level social skills. As you can imagine, these abilities will help your child through his entire life. Below is another activity for building your child's ability to master his emotions.

SURFING THE WAVES OF FEELINGS

The next exercise will help your child use the image of surfing, a fun and exciting sport, to help him manage his emotional sensitivity. He will learn how to go with the flow of his emotions. By doing this he will avoid two pitfalls of managing emotions: resistance and outbursts. A common mistake in dealing with emotions is trying to teach your child to resist his emotions through effort or willpower. But the more your child tries to resist a powerful emotion, the more likely he is to lose control. Resistance tends to make the emotion grow stronger and more primitive. Throw on top of that a feeling of failing to control the emotion, and resistance becomes like fuel to a fire.

EXERCISE: Stay with the Emotion

Ask your child to play a pretend game with you that will help him with his powerful emotions. Start by telling him (or reminding him) that his ADHD means that he has a special gift of emotional sensitivity, so he feels emotions more intensely than others do. Ask him to think about how we use the volume knob to turn the sound up or down on a TV or radio. Tell him that he is like a radio with the volume turned up high, which makes him more in tune with and more sensitive to the world and other people.

Explain that he needs to have special skills to manage his intense emotions so he can fit in at school and not get in trouble. Tell him that, like superheroes who have special abilities, he may sometimes struggle to fit in and need to develop strategies for getting along with others. Tell him that you will practice a pretend game to help him with this task: "Surfing the Waves of Emotion."

In this game he pretends that his emotions are waves. Tell him that, like waves, emotions tend to get bigger and bigger and then, right after they peak, they start to get smaller. Ask him to imagine his powerful emotions as waves and picture himself surfing a big wave. He can plan on the wave getting bigger, but if he just hangs on it will start to get smaller all by itself. He doesn't need to do anything; he just needs to imagine surfing a wave.

Now you can try the exercise. Have him think of a strong emotion he recently felt. Ask him to bring the emotion back, feeling it almost as strongly as he did then. Tell him to take a few deep breaths and to relax.

Next, ask him to pay attention to the emotion he's feeling and imagine surfing the wave of the emotion as it gets stronger. Like a surfer, he stays with the wave and rides it out as it gets smaller and eventually dies away. Remind him to stick with the feeling as it goes up and down and not try to jump away from it.

Practice this with your child daily on smaller, more manageable emotions. You might have more success with this exercise if you start out practicing in a calm setting before applying it in real settings. Tell your child that, like a surfer, he needs to practice on the smaller waves, but the real test will be when the big waves come. Talk with him about how he can remember to practice this when he is in school or when the waves seem really big. Develop strategies for him to remember to try surfing his emotions in other settings. The cards described below can serve as prompts that help your child remember to use this strategy in other settings.

Spend some time creating playful reminder cards. Take some blank index cards. Cut out magazine photos, or have your child draw pictures, of surfers, surfboards, big waves, or other images that evoke surfing. Paste these on one side of the blank cards. On the other side of the card, write a reminder affirmation. Here are some examples:

- Surf the wave.

- Stay with the feeling.

- Watch the wave get bigger.

- At the highest point, the wave will get smaller.

- Take a deep breath.

- Ride out the wave.

- You can surf the feeling.

- You can stay in control.

Keep track of how your child is using this strategy at school. Talk to him about when it seems to work and when it doesn't. Help him problem solve if there are specific obstacles. Remind him that the key to becoming a world-class surfer is "practice, practice, practice." Tell him not to get discouraged if it doesn't always work—even the best surfers wipe out on big waves and he will get better with practice.

The Problem with Resistance

It's common for frustrated parents to frame emotional outbursts as a moral failing. Parents may be tempted to express to a child that failure to control emotions is morally wrong because it involves defiance. This strategy will likely backfire, because the more you make your child feel wrong, the more negative emotions will pile up and the more unmanageable his emotions will become. One way of understanding this is the "container model" (Honos-Webb, Sunwolf, and Shapiro 2001). According to this model, you can think of each person as having a container that allows them to hold a certain amount of emotional experience. If too many powerful emotions fill the container, the person can no longer hold them, and a break-down of sorts occurs. In children, this breakdown looks like a temper tantrum. So if your child is already struggling with a powerful nega-tive emotion—for example, jealousy of a brother—and you tell him that the emotion is bad, he then has to contain the feeling of being jealous of his brother, the feeling of guilt about being jealous, and the feeling of sadness at being misunderstood. This is a recipe for a behavioral breakdown.

Thinking of your child with the container model in mind can help your understanding of him. Consider the following. A child's container is much smaller than an adult's, which means that behav-ior that would be terrible in an adult is often actually appropriate for a child. Not only is the child's container smaller—meaning that he has less capacity for tolerating emotions—but his brain is less developed. He cannot understand the world as well as an adult can, so he is more prone to being frustrated and experiencing negative emotion.

Imagine that you are at the bookstore with your son, Mark. Mark finds a thick science fiction book, which he pulls off the shelf and brings to you to buy for him. You know that the book is far beyond his reading level and that even if he could read it he wouldn't be interested in the subject matter. You tell him that the book is not appropriate for him and that you won't buy it for him. You point out that he has already picked out a book and that if he wants more he can pick some out at the library when you go there the next day. Mark starts to cry, saying that he wants this book and needs it now.

As you remain firm, Mark throws himself on the ground and has a temper tantrum, embarrassing you in the process.

Depending on how old your child is, this behavior may be perfectly predictable. For a younger child, the disappointment at not getting what he wants can be enormous. In addition, because his brain is not fully developed, he does not have as much capacity to hold back his emotional expression. On top of that, he isn't able to fully understand your logical explanation that he would not really enjoy or even use the book. His disappointment and frustration may be more than he can contain. As a parent, you are absolutely right to calmly persist in being firm by not buying the book. Over time these early disappointments serve to expand your child's capacity to contain disappointment. Not only are there real limits to what you can provide your child with, but he actually needs disappointments in order to build his capacity to tolerate future disappointments. So you do want to be firm, but you don't want to get mad at your child because his reactions are so immature. Children are immature by nature, and acting in the way described above is predictable for young children. The struggle for you as a parent is to increase your own capacity to tolerate your child's temper tantrums without punishing because of social embarrassment. Remember that, because of your child's interpersonal and emotional sensitivity, the angrier you become, the more your child will be tuned in to your anger. This sensitivity is more likely to bust his container, literally creating an outburst. And, the more he is punished, the worse he will feel about himself. This will fill up his container with bad feelings, making him incapable of tolerating other distressing emotions. This intolerance extends to even small disappointments like the one described above. Similarly, the more you give in to a temper tantrum, the less opportunity

> Not only are there real limits to what you can provide your child with, but he actually needs disappointments in order to build his capacity to tolerate future disappointments.

171

your child has to increase his capacity to tolerate disappointment and other negative emotions.

So how do you achieve this seemingly impossible task of remaining firm but not getting angry in the face of irrational, immature behavior? Many parents who have success with decreasing temper tantrums describe an episode that is a turning point, which I have come to call "The Showdown." It is a moment where a child pits his will against the parents' will—usually in a highly public place threatening a major meltdown. When a parent has lain down a rule such as "We're not buying any candy today," the child becomes determined to show who's boss and get the candy. Make no mistake—it will be much easier to just get your kid the candy than to stay strong. But this showdown is not at all about the candy—it's about who is in charge. If you can handle the showdown in the home many times, you may prevent it from happening in a public place. But chances are that your child will figure out that you cave in more easily in public places and test your will in one of these highly embarrassing situations. If you can win the showdown you will often notice a turning point. As in the alpha-male tests in the animal kingdom, the results of the showdown can be decisive—letting your child know that you really are in control.

The Problem with Outbursts

When you are helping your child manage his emotions, the second pitfall to avoid is to allow him to discharge his negative emotions by acting out in a disruptive way. It's important to recognize that, while you don't want to facilitate your child in resisting powerful emotion, neither do you want to facilitate negative behavior. You don't want to punish your child for outbursts, but you do want to direct him to more appropriate strategies for coping with intense emotions. The exercise below provides one such strategy that can serve as preventative medicine. It will help decrease the likelihood that your child will see only two options for dealing with emotions:

repress or act out. This third strategy will serve him for the rest of his life: staying with the emotion without acting it out.

THE CANARY IN THE COAL MINE

You may have become discouraged about your child's negative attitude toward school. You may be surprised to learn that scholars of education also do not agree with the current educational system and are calling for sweeping changes.

It has been argued that the current education system is an outdated model based on principles developed in the Industrial Revolution: children are like products, and schools are like factory assembly lines that use the same approach to assemble each product. The model has not accommodated the recent technological revolution and it does not accommodate the unique needs of individual students. As scholar Chris Yapp argues, "Education is the last model of Fordism—you put children on a conveyor belt at the age of four and let them fall off at different stages. From a quality viewpoint, they fall off at the point at which they fail. But you can choose your car, so why can't you have millions of national curriculums? Why not have a curriculum that meets the needs of each child?" (Fulton 1997, 69).

Even with the advent of the digital age, the current education system has not fully taken advantage of the many possibilities that technologies offer for transforming the way students learn. In one model, students could use current technologies and Internet resources to direct their own content areas and to gain technical expertise necessary for operating in a digital world.

Professor Brent Davies envisions a future in which children could engage in independent learning either in a school technology center or even at home (Fulton 1997). He argues that technologies such as the Internet, video conferencing, and educational software programs would allow for a comprehensive school program that would not require students to go to school five days a week. He also suggests that taking full advantage of technological innovation would reduce the burden on teachers, who are often underpaid and must work in overcrowded classrooms without adequate resources, due to budgetary constraints. Similarly, Chris Yapp has challenged our current expectations that a teacher be "guard, nanny, subject expert and administrator" (Fulton 1997, 69). Given the unrealistic demands and expectations put on teachers, it should come as no surprise that they are eager to find quick solutions to the problems wrought by children whose behavior is disruptive to class.

In short, your child's critical view of school is shared by forward-looking scholars. Your child's complaints may be less a symptom and more a perceptive summary of the current failings of an outmoded education system. All of this reflects your child's emotional sensitivity.

In past centuries, miners would carry a canary when they were working in mines, as a gauge of oxygen levels. Because canaries are more sensitive than humans, the canary would die first if there wasn't enough oxygen. If the canary died, the miners knew it was time to leave the mine. This metaphor can be applied to ADHD, because your child's difficulties in school may be seen as a warning sign not of an individual failing but of the failings of the education system.

The purpose of suggesting this metaphor is to help you to value your child's viewpoint about school. It does not mean that you should say, "Yeah, the education system is a mess, and it's all the teacher's fault that my child is struggling." However, it may give you a certain appreciation for your child's cogent perceptions of the school system and a sense that he really is not getting his needs met. As a parent, it's your responsibility to make sure your child gets those needs met, and there are several strategies you can use in handling your child's complaints.

Honoring Your Child's Complaints

One strategy is to avoid devaluing your child's complaints that his needs are not being met. In fact, you might want to encourage him to elaborate on his complaints in a constructive way. Ask him to identify how his needs are not being met at school, and write down what he says is not working. Some predictable complaints might be the following:

- The teacher is boring.

- I get in trouble for not sitting still.

- Nothing I learn has anything to do with the real world.

- Classes are boring.

- I'm more interested in other subjects.

- I want to play with the computers more.

- The worksheets are too much work.

- I get in trouble when I talk to other kids.

- I can't get help when I don't understand.

- School days are too long.

If your child's comments are like the ones above, then you will note that many of them are similar to the demands for change that are being made by scholars. So rather than getting mad at your child for not adapting to an outdated system, you can honor his complaints and then start to problem solve about how to get his needs met.

How to Get Your Child's Needs Met

Once you have the list of your child's unmet needs, begin to talk to him about what could be done to meet them. Let him talk about how he would solve the problem. He might come up with some creative ideas that you can put into action. He might realize that, with so many students and one teacher, it will be difficult to get every need met. What is important is that you show your child that you honor his needs and complaints. In this way, you're not attributing his problems to his diagnosis, and you can reframe for him the importance of his own experience.

BECOME AN EDUCATION REFORMER

As a parent, you probably haven't expected to have to become an activist just to see that your child receives the education he deserves. And perhaps you don't have to become a banner-waving, protest-attending activist. But by taking action to improve your child's experience at school, you are indeed being an activist—just of a quieter variety. So narrow down the list of your child's complaints to a few legitimate, actionable ones, and consider presenting these concerns to your child's teachers and principal. You can use many of the strategies you learned in chapter 4 on how to become your child's advocate rather than his apologist.

Like evolutionary mutations that help a species to survive, your child's intense sensitivity may help school administrators to recognize the dramatic changes that need to happen in the education system. These may be appealing to administrators, because some of the changes that were mentioned earlier actually have the potential to save resources. For example, allowing children to have self-directed learning sessions where they use computer and Internet resources to explore individualized topics of interest would meet the needs of both children and teachers: students could explore their own interests and teachers could have a break from trying to keep the attention of a large group of children on one topic. Although these suggestions may seem far-fetched given the bureaucratic systems of school districts, it seems worthwhile to envision a future where all sorts of neurocognitive differences are fully accepted and accommodated.

In the next chapter we will discuss some alternatives to a standard public school education. If your child is not succeeding in a setting that won't accommodate his unique gifts, you may want to consider an alternative educational setting. However, your child's sensitivity may give you an opportunity to work for change in the setting that needs to be changed—the traditional public schools.

Encouraging your child to join you in your crusade to transform the educational system can help utilize his gifts. His creativity and impatience can be fuel to generate ideas for changing the system, or at least changing things in his classroom. For example, on a smaller scale, he may propose fund-raisers to get more computers in school or suggest field trips to high-tech museums. His energy might be contagious to you and others.

KEEP THE CONNECTION

The most important benefit that will result from seeing your child as an intensely gifted and sensitive agent for change is the connection you will forge with him. Even if you don't succeed in making any changes in the structure of his education, you will succeed in showing him that you value his way of seeing the world. This is the single most important element in transforming your child's symptoms into gifts.

The main reason that children who are diagnosed with ADHD become increasingly difficult to manage in school and home settings is because their symptoms separate them emotionally from their parents. You can change this easily. If you emphasize connection over compliance, you can radically transform your child. More than anything, your child needs you. While it is perfectly predictable that parents will get angry and frustrated with children who won't comply, you have to remember that, even though it seems your child is pushing you away, he needs you to stay connected to him even in the face of his increasing independence.

It may help you to realize that your child's connection to you is not at all the same thing as compliance. As we discussed earlier in this book, sometimes what looks like defiance is actually self-reliance, and you can stay connected to your child by honoring his self-reliance. It seems like a paradox, but the more you honor his self-reliance, the more you connect with him because you're accepting him for who he is rather than trying to change him. A further paradox is that the more you honor your child's unique perceptions of the world, the more he will honor your need to set limits.

Out of all the exercises and strategies presented throughout this book, the most important one is to stay connected to your child. The more you can find a way to honor his differences, the more his behavior will be transformed. Children with ADHD get many complaints about their behavior, and it can be confusing. Some of their behavior simply represents their difference. Some of their behavior truly is inappropriate or defiant. Different behavior becomes bad behavior when children feel that they are being punished or feel disconnected from their parents. You may not always be sure when the behavior has crossed the line from different to bad. In either case, the more you can stay connected, the more you will decrease bad behavior and increase your child's willingness to honor your perceptions and needs.

SUMMARY

This chapter reviewed the way in which symptoms of ADHD can be seen as a form of intense emotional sensitivity. Your child's sensitivity can be seen as a gift, increasing his capacity to create and to connect with others. One strategy for helping your child preserve his sensitivity and maintain socially appropriate behavior is to encourage him to ask for help when he finds his emotions getting out of control. This strategy gives your child permission to admit that he cannot control his emotions while giving him a technique for learning on-the-spot methods for effectively handling social situations. The chapter also offered specific techniques for monitoring and managing emotions as they emerge.

> A further paradox is that the more you honor your child's unique perceptions of the world, the more he will honor your need to set limits.

CHAPTER 10

How to Navigate the Educational and Mental Health Systems

As a parent of a child with ADHD, you may now have a new perspective on your child, and you may be experiencing a whole range of thoughts and feelings. Perhaps you are heartened by this new perspective. You might be saying that you have thought your child was uniquely gifted but unappreciated all along. You may have found yourself charmed by your child at times and annoyed at other times, when you thought that her behavior was part of her ADHD symptoms. You may have even hidden your affection for your child's irreverence, fearing that you might encourage bad behavior.

The main point of this book can be summarized in two major principles: your positive perceptions of your child will transform her; your close connection with your child will transform her.

Because your child is so sensitive and interpersonally intuitive, she knows exactly how you are evaluating her and is particularly attuned to your reactions to her. You cannot hide your feelings from her. The more you can view her in positive ways, the more she will internalize that perception and act it out. The power of the self-fulfilling prophecy cannot be underestimated.

This power means that your expectations for your child will create those very same qualities. Research has demonstrated that teachers' expectations for students' performance comes to have powerful effects in creating the behavior they expected to see (Rosenthal 1987). This phenomenon is much more powerful for parents and children. The good news is that your expectations for your child have a lot of power to transform her. On the other hand, as a parent you may need to label your child in order to gain access to accommodations in the school system. With appropriate confidentiality within the school, you can balance the need for positive perceptions of your child and the need for an environment in which your child will thrive.

The premise of this book, that your child has a difference that is a gift and not a disorder, has the power to transform her life. You need only to convey this powerful expectation to your child, and she will absorb it like a sponge. As your expectations change, so will your ability to connect with your child. The more you connect with your child, the more dramatic a transformation you can expect to see.

When children with ADHD behave badly, it is usually because they feel badly about themselves. Children with ADHD feel poorly about themselves in part because of

> The main point of this book can be summarized in two major principles: your positive perceptions of your child will transform her; your close connection with your child will transform her.

the extreme emphasis on school achievement over all other talents and interests. One psychologist attributes the high rates of depression that accompany learning disorders to this emphasis: "In our modern technological society, where education is more important and more highly valued than ever, academic achievement and school-related intelligence have attained an importance that is probably far greater than ever before" (Migden 2002, 155).

By conveying to your child that the label of ADHD means she has a gift, you can turn around both of these causes of bad behavior. As your child learns to value her difference, she will not need to act out her sense of inferiority or frustration. Also, if you can maintain your sense of closeness with your child, even in the face of apparently bad behavior, your child will no longer need to act out her sense of being alienated.

Just by transforming your vision of your child from disordered to gifted, you can facilitate a dramatic transformation in her. While it is predictable that parents of children with ADHD will at times feel anger, impatience, and frustration with their child, you can channel these feelings toward the culture's intolerance of your child's gift. You yourself can be transformed into a social activist as you become aware of how your child has been underserved by the current medical model and a failing educational system.

COPING WITH THE REST OF THE WORLD

As you come to appreciate your child's gifts, you may find yourself continually frustrated by how little your new perspective is shared in the real world. There are three strategies for coping with others' attitudes toward your child. One is to transform your own negative emotional responses toward others' rejecting attitudes. Another is to become an advocate for your child in mental health and educational settings. Another is to find alternative treatments and educational settings that respect your child's difference as a gift.

> These findings also indicate a powerful truth about your child's symptoms: your own level of functioning dramatically affects your child's symptoms.

All of these strategies include your remaining active in your efforts to cope with your child's diagnosis of ADHD. The worst thing you can do is to give up and give in to feeling hopeless and helpless, which can lead to depression and lessen your child's likelihood of improvement. And recent research has found that children diagnosed with ADHD have a poorer response to medication when their primary care provider reports depressive symptoms: "Our findings suggest that consideration of parental psychological adjustment may be key when treating children with medication. Initial screening of parents for depressive symptoms, followed by treatment for those who are at least mildly depressed, might result in more children with ADHD showing excellent response to treatments that are medication based" (Owens et al. 2003, 549).

These findings suggest that when you feel hopeless it is important for you and for your child's recovery that you seek treatment for yourself. These findings also indicate a powerful truth about your child's symptoms: your own level of functioning dramatically affects your child's symptoms. However, by remaining active in your coping efforts, you have the power to prevent depression.

Transform Your Feelings

While it is predictable that at times you will feel hopeless, helpless, angry, frustrated, and filled with despair, it is also important that you find effective strategies for coping with these feelings. As you do with your child, validate and honor these feelings but learn not to become overwhelmed by them. You can try the exercise in chapter 9 called "Stay with the Emotion" with your own feelings about your child's behavior and diagnosis. For example, if you have to face yet another teacher making complaints about your child's behavior in class, you may feel a sense of despair clouding your mind.

But you don't want to repress the feeling and pretend everything is okay. Neither do you want to just give in to it, go to bed, and pull the covers over your head. You, too, can surf it out. You will find that when you allow yourself to feel the despair and let it peak in intensity, it will subside.

When you feel despair or hopelessness to its full power, you may find that the experience not only lessens the emotion but transforms into a radically different experience. Psychologist Alvin Mahrer calls this transformation of fully experienced emotion "the deeper potential of experiencing" (2004). The activity below will help you transform negative feelings.

EXERCISE: From Despairing to Empowered

This exercise is inspired by *The Complete Guide to Experiential Psychotherapy* (Mahrer 2004).

Identify a time when you are feeling hopeless or helpless. Typically, you may respond to this feeling by trying to distract yourself from it or push it away. Instead, try to amplify the feeling by making it stronger and more intense. For example, you can allow the feeling of helplessness to turn into a feeling of complete paralysis or allow the hopelessness to turn into a feeling of complete doom and gloom.

As the feeling becomes more intense, try to find a specific memory or image that triggered it. For example, maybe you got another complaining call from the teacher, and you found yourself dwelling on the image of the teacher possibly sneering at you on the other end of the phone line and thinking you are the worst parent in the world.

Now imagine that you are the teacher. Try to feel the teacher's power and superior attitude toward you. Amplify your feeling that the teacher has the authority to pass judgments. Make the teacher's feelings stronger. Imagine that the teacher is all powerful, the one who knows, the one who has the right to tell you how to understand your child. Follow your imagination in elaborating on this role.

Take this new feeling of being menacing, threatening, or empowered, and own it for yourself. Practice feeling like you are the judge. Now, turn it around and tell the teacher that she is failing your child. Imagine telling the teacher that she does not understand your child. Practice owning this feeling of power and authority. You will want to use your judgment in how you will apply this new feeling in taking action in the real world, but you can use this technique to transform your feelings of powerlessness and despair.

Active Approaches to Transforming Helplessness

As noted above, you may be able to prevent depression by becoming an advocate for your child and trying to create change in her existing environments. Throughout this book, and specifically in chapter 4, we discussed strategies for becoming an advocate and not an apologist for your child. In chapter 9, it was suggested that you might even need to become a social activist in advocating for educational reform to meet your child's needs. If this approach is not your style, consider another approach for getting your child's needs met: finding alternative environments.

MENTAL HEALTH TREATMENT OPTIONS

Because some people might consider behavioral health interventions themselves to be alternative health options, this section will clarify a continuum of alternatives to medication for ADHD symptoms.

Review of the Standard Treatment Approach

According to 1990s research on ADHD, the best approach to alleviating symptoms, including poor academic performance and family relations, is to combine medication and intensive behavior therapy (MTA Cooperative Group 1999). While research shows that in the short term this approach has benefits, the follow-up of this same gold standard research program discovered that in the long term—after eight years—there are no differences between students who initially received medication and those who did not (MTA Study Group 2009). The standard treatment for ADHD is none-theless medication prescribed by a pediatrician or child psychiatrist, who monitors its dosage and effects on a regular basis.

As described in chapter 1, treating ADHD with medication has costs and benefits. The benefit is that research has shown that it is the most effective treatment for quickly reducing symptoms of ADHD in children in the short term. Among the many drawbacks of medications, besides the possible lack of long-term effectiveness, mentioned above, is the concern that there is no research on their long-term effects on children. Additionally, recent research on the effects of these stimulants on the brain (in animal studies) suggests the risk that long-term use of stimulants can lead to depression, anxiety, and cognitive deficits (Higgens 2009).

Alternative treatments for ADHD are increasingly available. These resources offer a great deal of hope to parents and can be used in addition to or in place of medication, if appropriate. These avail-able resources may also make your job more difficult, as you have to consider the time, money, and energy they require. Unfortunately, the research on alternative ADHD treatments is not strong enough to offer clear recommendations based only on the empirical evi-dence. Given that the research is not extensive on even the standard medical treatment, it's not surprising that there is even less research on alternative treatments. Consequently, it can be difficult to decide which treatments to try.

Additional Treatments

Parent coaching may be essential to support your child's level of functioning. You can connect with a therapist who will help you address specific strategies for working with your child. This may entail helping you foster emotional intelligence in your child, improve communications skills, and manage your child's challenges.

Another treatment choice is family therapy. By working with the whole family, a therapist can help manage stressors, address conflicts, and solve problems. As these problems are resolved and as the family gains more skills for finding specific solutions, the child's level of functioning is likely to improve.

Individual play therapy for younger children, or counseling for older children, can lead to improvements. Because of the emotional sensitivity of ADHD children, having a safe place to release and heal emotions can decrease symptoms. Children may gain from building emotional intelligence and learning stress management and other coping techniques. Cognitive therapy, used to overcome negative attitudes, can increase motivation and confidence, thereby improving the child's level of functioning.

CONFIRM THE DIAGNOSIS

Before launching into a full-scale effort at using every treatment available, however, a first step would be to make sure you have at least a second opinion to confirm the diagnosis of ADHD. Research has shown that the first suggestion of ADHD more often comes from teachers than from parents, physicians, or others (Sax and Kautz 2003). Teachers' perceptions may be influenced by their own heavy workload, classes that are too large, and access to too few resources. Sometimes pediatricians and psychiatrists rely on the referral of parents and teachers without conducting a thorough assessment themselves. Because the symptoms of ADHD overlap extensively with normal developmental behaviors and other clinical disorders, it is important that a thorough assessment be conducted before a diagnosis of ADHD is made. The diagnosis of ADHD requires a full range of symptoms present in more than one setting and usually entails checklists being filled out by both teachers and parents. For example, a child can be disruptive in class and not meet the full criteria for ADHD. In this case, she should not be treated using medication. Before expending time and energy treating ADHD, take the preliminary steps of confirming the diagnosis through a psychiatrist or psychologist who is trained in thorough assessment of this particular disorder. An ideal evaluator would be a pediatric neuropsychologist.

OTHER CAUSES OF ADHD-LIKE SYMPTOMS

Children can show ADHD-like symptoms for many reasons other than having the actual disorder. For example, children may be disruptive because they are under too much stress. There may be family problems that they are acting out at school. A child who has suffered a recent loss (the illness or death of a parent, a grandparent, or a sibling) can be expected to show disturbance in her behavior. These disruptions will pass if the child is given a chance to talk about and receive support for her concerns. A child may show ADHD-like symptoms because one parent is depressed or because there is serious marital conflict between her parents.

If your child does not have a long-standing history of hyperactivity and attention problems but developed symptoms suddenly, then you should suspect some reaction to life events. Ask yourself whether any major, life-changing events recently occurred in your family prior to the appearance of ADHD-like symptoms:

- Did a parent lose a job?

- Has your child had health problems?

- Have there been health problems in family members?

- Have there been any deaths in the family?

- Have there been serious marital conflicts?

- Have any older siblings left the home?

- Has there been any physical, emotional, or sexual abuse?

- Is either parent depressed or anxious?

- Are there legal problems in the family?

- Are there serious financial problems in the family?

- Does either parent use or abuse alcohol or drugs?

Children are dramatically affected by these kinds of events, and it is predictable that their behavior will change to act out their fears, losses, anger, and stress. If you answered yes to any of the preceding questions, and your child's behavioral problems seemed to develop suddenly rather than being present for a long time, you might want to consider that your child does not have ADHD at all. In that case, the appropriate approach would be a form of supportive treatment. This would give her an opportunity to fully talk through her concerns and get support, and her behavior problems would very likely subside.

Because the diagnosis of ADHD is unreliable and because the symptoms overlap with so many other diagnoses (such as depression, anxiety, and Asperger's disorder), I now recommend that a child receive twelve sessions of therapy before getting an assessment of ADHD. In this way, the clinician and family can work to reduce the symptoms of stress and be able to determine what is really a brain difference and what is really the behavior of a young child coping with stressors or other clinical problems. This can prevent the assignment of a label of ADHD, which can follow a child into adulthood and throughout his life. It is also important to keep in mind that ADHD is not an either/or condition like pregnancy (either you are pregnant or you are not). Many clinicians agree that ADHD exists on a continuum and many people have some of the ADHD symptoms some of the time.

As a parent you should understand that most psychologists are trained to think in terms of normal versus disorder, diagnosis or no diagnosis. The problem with this worldview is that, as mentioned above, many people have traits and temperaments that look like ADHD but do not add up to clinical disorders. Many children are highly active and seek stimulation by trait and temperament. This is a normal personality expression, not a clinical disorder. Some kids learn through touch and movement rather than by passively taking in abstract knowledge. This is not a clinical disorder but rather one of many different learning styles. If your child has a temperament that looks like ADHD, it is important for you to remember that the diagnosis of ADHD is a bona fide mental illness. Although the word gets used in some circles like a new fad, don't be flip about the possible stigma attached to the label. If you think your child has a temperament that looks like ADHD but is not a disorder, consider reading two excellent books, *When the Labels Don't Fit* (2008) by Barbara Probst and *Please Don't Label My Child* (2007) by Dr. Scott Shannon.

If the problems your child is reacting to are deep-seated family conflicts, then you should seek family therapy for the whole family or couples therapy for you and your partner. If one parent is suffering from depression or another mental health disorder, including the abuse of drugs or alcohol, then that parent should seek individual treatment for the problem.

As we have stressed throughout this book, the most effective way of handling reality-based distress of your child, whether you use supportive therapy or not, is to stay connected to her and offer to talk with her about her concerns. The more you can hear her feelings, accept them, offer her honest feedback, and reassure her, the more she will be able to tolerate life stressors.

If the root problems, including reactions to life-changing events and family conflict, are not addressed and your child is given medication to control her symptoms without getting necessary therapeutic support, she may be at risk for developing long-standing behavioral problems. One reason for this is that she may never learn how to tolerate and work through the existential complications of life. As concluded by one scholar, "Suppressing these symptoms by 'subduing' the child with medication hides from all the source of the child's troubles, precludes his being able to obtain mastery of his troubles through understanding, and subjects him to a false label of brain pathology" (Furman 2002, 141).

If you recognize that any of the stressors listed above is present, you don't need to feel guilty or that you're to blame. Family problems are a perennial fact of life. You are not bad if you are depressed or have a serious conflict with your spouse. Marital conflict, depression, anxiety, and professional setbacks can be expected to occur in any human life. Your child needs to be exposed to these difficulties and needs to receive support in dealing with them. You can think of this process as being similar to the way your child developed her immune system. Every child needs to be exposed to illness, get sick, and fight it off in order to develop a strong immune system. Similarly, you cannot protect your child from all of life's trials and tribulations. The more she can work through her feelings and learn how to cope with difficult life events, the more she will be prepared to cope with her own challenges as she grows more independent. A child may have both ADHD and several stressors, so a thorough evaluation is necessary in order to sort out a correct diagnosis for your child.

MEDITATION

More stress equals less attention. Consequently, if you reduce your child's stress you will increase his attention. One of the most important things you can do to build your child's attention is to teach him to manage his own stress. Below are some quick tips.

- The fastest way to reduce stress is to practice deep, relaxing breaths. Teaching your child simply to pay attention to his breath can begin the process of relaxation.

- A simple practice of meditation in which your child focuses his attention on a relaxing phrase or word for ten minutes a day can serve the dual purpose of helping him to relax and actually building your child's capacity to pay attention. Just like your child can build muscles by lifting weights, so can he build his attention, by daily practice.

- You can help your child practice physical relaxation by tensing and releasing his muscles. It can be as simple as reminding him to raise his shoulders to his ears for five seconds and then release. Next, he can tense his hands into fists and then release. Move through each of the major muscles one at a time. This will help him begin to learn to control his level of physical stress.

ALTERNATIVE EDUCATIONAL OPTIONS

In addition to exploring alternative mental health treatment options, consider investigating educational alternatives that may help in transforming your child. The reasons for doing so are many. Statistically, children with ADHD will have many failure experiences in educational settings, including a 33 percent chance of being held back one year in school, with up to 35 percent of children diagnosed failing to complete high school (Barkley 2000). While there is little conclusive and consistent research on how the environment in school settings affects outcome, Russell Barkley (2000), a leading researcher, outlines certain features of an educational setting that are likely to lead to positive outcomes for your child. His summarized conclusions are below:

- Positive outcomes are more likely if you increase novelty and stimulation, including color, shape, and texture, to enhance attention and increase performance.

- Tasks should be of high interest to the child and active rather than passive. "Tasks requiring an active as opposed to a passive response may also allow children with ADHD to better channel their disruptive behaviors into constructive responses" (236).

- Brief lessons with the child as an active participant will increase persistence.

- Tasks and lessons should include physical exercise to increase attention span.

- Positive outcomes are more likely if you include hands-on, direct-instruction materials, like computers with software that promotes content learning.

If you can advocate for these changes in your child's current educational system, you will be helping your child. As noted in chapter 9, these changes are similar to those advocated by educational scholars who argue that the current educational system is outdated and does not meet the needs of children of the digital age.

There are alternative, private educational settings that emphasize these forms of teaching and are most consonant with the needs of a child diagnosed with ADHD. But not all expensive private schools will be the best match for your child. For example, many private college-preparatory schools will emphasize discipline, achievement, and a form of education least suited to the needs of a child with ADHD. In contrast, some independent private schools and even a few public magnet or charter schools accommodate different styles of learning and emphasize the independence of the child. Regardless of whether you are looking at private or public schools, you will want to find one whose philosophy is consistent with the key principles listed above, such as individualized attention to your child, high levels of activity, and relative emphasis on your child's independent learning.

The Montessori Method

In addition to researching the philosophies of individual schools, you can look into schools with certain widely used instructional methods. One example of a teaching method that seems ideally suited to children with ADHD is the Montessori method (Montessori 1967; 1966). All of the elements of an ideal educational setting listed by Barkley are fundamental to the Montessori method.

INDIVIDUALIZED LESSONS

The Montessori method uses individualized teaching methods rather than teaching a single lesson to a larger group. Maria Montessori writes that in an ideal teaching method the teacher "should refrain from letting the child know that he has made a mistake or has not understood, since this might arrest for a long time the impulse to act, which constitutes the whole basis for progress" (1967, 107). As this quotation illustrates, the Montessori method is very different from standardized educational approaches. The methods are most suited to a child who needs individualized attention and easily gets lost in group lessons that require focused concentration on abstract concepts. In the Montessori method, the child chooses independent learning tasks based on her own needs and special interests.

MEETING THE NEED FOR PHYSICAL ACTIVITY

Central to the Montessori method is the understanding that, for children, learning requires physical movement. A child's mind is not yet fully rational and abstracted from her body, and she learns through action and moving in the world. As Maria Montessori writes about physical activity, "Everybody admits that a child must be constantly on the move. This need for movement, which is irresistible in childhood, apparently diminishes with the development of inhibiting forces at the time when these, by entering into a harmony with the motor impulses, create the means for subjecting them to the will" (79). This emphasis on allowing movement and offering sensory-based tasks as methods for learning is ideally suited to the child diagnosed with ADHD.

Also implicit in the Montessori method is that individualized instruction that involves lots of movement may prevent the symptoms of ADHD from plaguing a child throughout her life. Maria Montessori seems to imply in this quotation and in other writings that if a child is allowed to learn through individualized attention and movement, she will internalize and develop the "inhibiting forces" that are the basis of discipline and concentration. Many authors

193

have characterized ADHD as a failure to inhibit oneself. This line of reasoning leads to the radical and troubling possibility that the high rates of ADHD symptoms could be caused in part by educational methods that do not allow the full expression of the need for physical activity. If children are prohibited from meeting their need for movement, they may not enter into "harmony with the motor impulses"—which Montessori argues is the very means for "subjecting them to the will" and learning how to inhibit themselves.

FOCUS ON SENSORY LEARNING

One of the fundamental principles of the Montessori method is an emphasis on the child's engagement with the concrete, sensory world. There is little to no emphasis on grasping abstract knowledge. Rather, children in Montessori schools play and learn with concrete sensory objects of many different shapes and textures, not through standardized group lessons. For example, children play with movable letters of the alphabet, each with a different texture, to learn the fundamentals of reading. They can see the letters while also feeling their shapes and textures. At higher levels, children play with blocks to learn the fundamentals of mathematic manipulations. They handle and move the blocks in conjunction with learning about numbers, adding, and subtracting.

As emphasized throughout this book, a child with ADHD needs to learn through active engagement of her senses. As you can see, the Montessori method may be an appropriate match to this need. Again, there is also the suggestion that the lack of sensory education in standardized educational systems may play a role in creating ADHD-like symptoms. Maria Montessori writes, "[w]hen a fugitive mind fails to find something upon which it may work, it becomes absorbed with images and symbols. Children who are afflicted with this disorder move restlessly about. They are lively, irrepressible, but without purpose. They start something only to leave it unfinished, since their energies are directed toward many different objects without being able to settle upon any of them" (1966, 155).

The implication is that if a child's inherent need to engage the sensory world is denied through emphasis on abstract learning, then symptoms of hyperactivity and difficulty in concentrating may result. Maria Montessori writes that if these symptoms have already developed, an education focused on direct sensory engagement with the environment and physical activity will lead to dramatic changes in the child's capacity for discipline and concentration.

As you can see, the method of education your child receives can have a direct impact on her symptoms of ADHD. Maria Montessori's method suggests that the best education for any child is one that allows for individualized rather than group lessons, encourages physical activity, and focuses on sensory engagement with concrete objects rather than learning abstracted knowledge and facts. Her writing hints at the idea that if a child is denied these fundamental needs, symptoms that look like ADHD may develop.

APPLYING THE METHOD

If you do not have access to a Montessori school, you can become an advocate for incorporating these elements of learning into your child's current educational experience. You can also incorporate your understanding of the inherent needs of children into your parenting style.

One simple adjustment you can make is to reframe your child's constant activity as representing an inherent need rather than disobedience. Maria Montessori suggests that children learn to inhibit behavior by connecting their mind and their body through active physical engagement with the environment. Thus, you may want to encourage and validate your child's need for constant movement. It's easy to get frustrated with your child's need to touch everything in the environment and see this behavior as a distraction from focused activity. But the more you can allow your child to engage with the environment in accord with her own interests, the more she will harmoniously connect her body and mind. The more words and abstract teaching she is subjected to, the more she may experience a disconnect between her mind and body. In some way, this takes a lot of pressure off of you as a parent. Rather than feeling that you have to provide knowledge to your child, you can shift your emphasis to permitting and allowing her exploration of her sensory environment. A child may benefit more from playing with pegs and a board with holes of different sizes and shapes than from listening to you explain the difference between a circle and a square.

SUMMARY

This chapter talked about how to approach the educational and mental health professionals who work with your child, and how to make sure she receives the right kind of education and therapeutic support. We discussed how your perception of your child can make all the difference in how she functions in school and at home. By staying connected with her all the time, you will help her transform her ADHD symptoms into strengths. This chapter also offered strategies for coping with the "real world," in which the perceptions of your child will not be informed by the new vision you have gained. Specific strategies were provided for interacting with the mental health systems and educational systems in which your child participates.

References

Abram, D. 1996. *The Spell of the Sensuous*. New York: Pantheon Books.

American Psychiatric Association. 2000. *Diagnostic and Statistical Manual of Mental Disorders (DSM-IV)*. 4th ed. Washington, DC: American Psychiatric Association.

Arye, L. 2001. *Unintentional Music: Releasing Your Deepest Creativity*. Charlottesville, VA: Hampton Roads.

Barkley, R. A. 2000. *Taking Charge of ADHD: The Complete Authoritative Guide for Parents*. New York: Guilford.

Berman, M. G., J. Jonides, and S. Kaplan. 2008. The cognitive benefits of interacting with nature. *Psychological Science* 19:1207–12.

Breggin, P. R., and D. Cohen. 1999. *Your Drug May Be Your Problem: How and Why to Stop Taking Psychiatric Medications.* Reading, MA: Perseus Books.

Charles, C., R. Louv, L. Bodner, and B. Gung. 2008. *Children and Nature 2008: A Report on the Movement to Reconnect Children to the Natural World.* Santa Fe, NM: Children and Nature Network.

Faber-Taylor, A. F., F. E. Kuo, and W. C. Sullivan. 2001. Coping with ADD: The surprising connection to green play settings. *Environment and Behavior* 33:54–77.

————. 2002. Views of nature and self-discipline: Evidence from inner-city children. *Journal of Environmental Psychology* 22:49–63.

Freud, S. 1963. *Therapy and Technique.* New York: Collier.

Fulton, K. 1997. *Learning in a Digital Age: Insights into the Issues.* College Park, MD: Center for Learning and Educational Technology, University of Maryland.

Furman, R. A. 2002. Attention deficit/hyperactivity disorder: An alternative viewpoint. *Journal of Infant, Child and Adolescent Psychotherapy* 2:125–44.

Gardner, H. 1999. *Intelligence Reframed: Multiple Intelligences for the Twenty-First Century.* New York: Basic Books.

Glausiusz, J. 2009. Devoted to distraction. *Psychology Today,* March–April, 84–91.

Goldstein, R. 2002. *The Parenting Bible: The Answers to Parents' Most Common Questions.* Naperville, IL: Sourcebooks.

Goleman, D. 2009. *Ecological Intelligence.* New York: Broadway Books.

Groth-Marnat, G. 2003. *Handbook of Psychological Assessment.* 4th ed. New York: Wiley.

Hartmann, T. 1997. *Attention Deficit Disorder: A Different Perception.* Grass Valley, CA: Underwood Books.

Higgens, E. S. 2009. Do ADHD drugs take a toll on the brain? *Scientific American Mind,* July–August, 38–43.

Hillman, J. 1983. *Healing Fiction.* New York: Station Hill.

Hillman, J., and M. Ventura. 1992. *We've Had a Hundred Years of Psychotherapy and the World's Getting Worse.* New York: Harper Collins.

Honos-Webb, L., Sunwolf, and J. L. Shapiro. 2001. Toward the re-enchantment of psychotherapy: Stories as container. *Humanistic Psychologist* 29:70–97.

Hoza, B., W. E. Pelham, D. A. Waschbusch, H. Kipp, and J. S. Owens. 2001. Academic task persistence of normally achieving ADHD and control boys: Performance, self-evaluations, and attributions. *Journal of Consulting and Clinical Psychology* 69:271–83.

Leitner, L. M., A. J. Faidley, and M. A. Celentana. 2000. Diagnosing human meaning making: An experiential constructivist approach. In *Constructions of Disorder: Meaning-Making Frameworks for Psychotherapy,* edited by R. A. Neimeyer and J. D. Raskin. Washington, DC: American Psychological Association.

Louv, R. 2005. *Last Child in the Woods: Saving Our Children from Nature-Deficit Disorder.* Chapel Hill, NC: Algonquin.

Mahrer, A. R. 2004. *The Complete Guide to Experiential Psychotherapy.* Boulder, CO: Bull Publishing Company.

Migden, S. 2002. Self-esteem and depression in adolescents with specific learning disability. *Journal of Infant, Child and Adolescent Psychotherapy* 2:145–60.

Montessori, M. 1966. *The Secret of Childhood.* New York: Ballantine.

————. 1967. *The Discovery of the Child*. New York: Ballantine.

Mooney, J., and D. Cole. 2000. *Learning Outside the Lines*. New York: Fireside.

MTA Cooperative Group. 1999. A fourteen-month randomized clinical trial of treatment strategies for attention-deficit/hyperactivity disorder. *Archives of General Psychiatry* 56:1073–86.

MTA Study Group. 2009. The MTA at eight years: Prospective follow-up of children treated for combined-type ADHD in a multisite study. *Journal of the American Academy of Child and Adolescent Psychiatry* 48:484–500.

Nadis, S. 2004. In the line of fire. *Astronomy*, January, 42–47.

Owens, E. B., S. P. Hinshaw, H. C. Kraemer, L. E. Arnold, H. B. Abikoff, D. P. Cantwell, C. K. Conners, et al. 2003. Which treatment for whom for ADHD? Moderators of treatment response in the MTA. *Journal of Consulting and Clinical Psychology* 71:540–52.

Owens, J. S., and B. Hoza. 2003. The role of inattention and hyperactivity/impulsivity in the positive illusory bias. *Journal of Consulting and Clinical Psychology* 71:680–91.

Pink, D. H. 2005. *A Whole New Mind*. New York: Penguin.

Probst, B. 2008. *When the Labels Don't Fit*. New York: Three Rivers Press.

Psychological Corporation. 1997. *WAIS-III/WMS-III Technical Manual*. San Antonio, TX: Psychological Corporation.

Rosenthal, R. 1987. Pygmalion effects: Existence, magnitude, and social importance. *Educational Researcher* 16:37–41.

Ruffman, T., L. Slade, and E. Crowe. 2002. The relation between children's and mothers' mental state language and theory-of-mind understanding. *Child Development* 73:734–51.

Sax, L., and K. J. Kautz. 2003. Who first suggests the diagnosis of Attention-Deficit/Hyperactivity Disorder? *Annals of Family Medicine* 1:171–74.

Schultz, M. 1999. *Awakening Intuition: Using Your Mind-Body Network for Insight and Healing.* New York: Three Rivers Press.

Shannon, S. M. 2007. *Please Don't Label My Child.* New York: Rodale.

Siegel, D. J. 2007. *The Mindful Brain: Reflections and Attunement in the Cultivation of Well-Being.* New York: Norton.

Stein, D. B. 1999. *Ritalin Is Not the Answer: A Drug-Free, Practical Program for Children Diagnosed with ADD or ADHD.* San Francisco: Jossey-Bass.

Tennessen, C. M., and B. Cimprich. 1995. Views to Nature: Effects on attention. *Journal of Environmental Psychology* 15:77–85.

VanKuiken, D. A. 2004. Meta-analysis of the effect of guided imagery practice on outcomes. *Journal of Holistic Nursing* 22:164–79.

Volkow, N. 2006. Prescription stimulants—Retaining the benefits while mitigating the abuse risk. *Child and Adolescent Psychopharmacology News*, Guilford Publications 11 (3): 1–4.

Walsh, B. 2009. Ten ideas changing the world right now. *Time*, March 23.

Yuill, N., S. Sullivan, T. Ruffman, and L. Slade. 2007. Continuity from three to eleven years in children's theory of mind and mental state talk. Conference presentation for the European Society for Developmental Psychology, Jena, Germany.

Lara Honos-Webb, Ph.D., is a clinical psychologist licensed in California. She is also author of *Listening to Depression: How Understanding Your Pain Can Heal Your Life*, which was selected by *Health* magazine as one of the best therapy books of 2006; *The Gift of ADHD Activity Book: 101 Ways to Transform Problems into Strengths*; and *The Gift of Adult ADD.* Her work has been featured in newspapers, on websites, and on radio and television stations across the country, including *Newsweek*, the *Wall Street Journal*, the *Chicago Tribune, Publishers Weekly*, ivillage.com, msn.com, and abcnews.com. More than one hundred and twenty-five thousand copies of her books are in print. The American Psychiatric Association included *The Gift of ADHD* (2005) as recommended reading in the "ADHD Parents Medication Guide."

She specializes in the treatment of ADHD and depression and the psychology of pregnancy and motherhood; she speaks regularly on her areas of expertise. She hosts a popular podcast show, "The Sweet Spot." She completed a two-year postdoctoral research fellowship at University of California, San Francisco, and has been an assistant professor teaching graduate students. She has published more than twenty-five scholarly articles. Visit her website at www.visionarysoul .com.

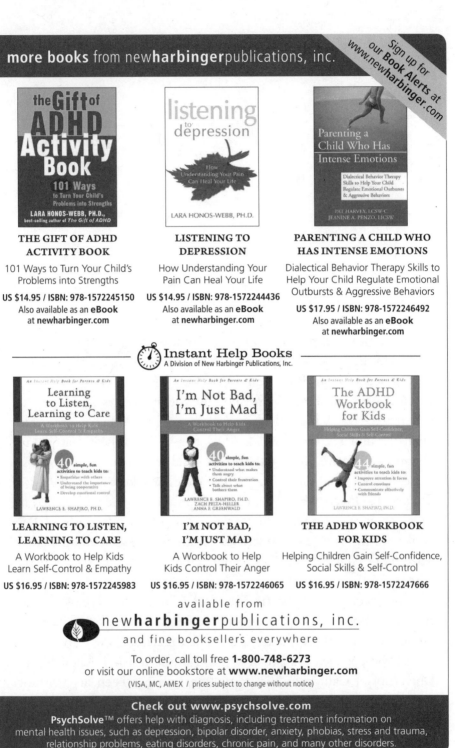